CALVARY CHAPEL DISTINCTIVES

Calvary Chapel Distinctives
by Chuck Smith

Copyright © 2000, 2001 by The Word For Today Publishers,
P.O. Box 8000, Costa Mesa, CA 92628.

Web site: www.twft.com
E-mail: info@twft.com

ISBN 0-936728-80-9

TABLE OF CONTENTS

PREFACE

What is it that makes Calvary Chapel different from other Bible-believing, evangelical churches? It's always good to have a grasp of the unique work that God has done in our fellowship. If Calvary Chapel is exactly like the church across the street it would be better to simply merge the two. But, if there are distinctives that make us different, then we have a unique and special place in the plan of God. Certainly there are churches that share many of our beliefs and practices. We're not renegades. But God has done a wonderful work of balance in the Calvary Chapel movement that does make us different in many areas.

There are many who believe in the gifts and the ministry of the Holy Spirit, but they don't have a strong emphasis on Biblical teaching, nor do they look to the Word to guide their experiences with the Holy Spirit. There are many who have a strong emphasis on teaching the Word of God, but they don't share the view that the gifts of the Holy Spirit are available and valid today. In Calvary Chapel we find the teaching of the Word, and an open heart to the work of the Holy Spirit. It is this balance that makes Calvary Chapel a distinct and uniquely blessed movement of God. And so

1

it's important to understand the Biblical principles that make up the picture of why God has allowed us to exist and grow.

This is not to say that all Calvary Chapels are identical. I'm always amazed at how God can take simple basic elements and create such variety out of them. Basically, all of us have two eyes, a nose, a mouth, and two ears, and yet how different we all look from each other! People also have different emotional make-ups. Now, God loves everyone. He loves the highly emotional and He loves the dull and unemotional. In the same way, wanting all men to be able to relate to Him, God created a wide variety of churches. Some churches appeal to those who are very emotional in their nature while others appeal to a more staid and formal personality. God, desiring to reach and bless all kinds of people, seems to enjoy having a wide variety of churches so that everybody's needs might be met, from the highly emotional to the very formal, and all those in between. Each of us has a part to play in God's plan, but we all need to know where we fit in this wide spectrum. That is why it's crucial for us to grasp what we call the Calvary Chapel Distinctives. As we see what makes our fellowship unique, we will also come to better understand our position in the body of Christ.

THE CALL TO THE MINISTRY

"No man taketh this honour unto himself, but he that is called of God..."
Heb. 5:4

Before we look at what we call the *"Calvary Chapel Distinctives"*, let's first consider the vital subject of our calling and commitment to the ministry.

If there is one characteristic that is absolutely essential for effective ministry, it's that we must first have a sense of calling—the conviction in our hearts that God has chosen and called us to serve Him. The Bible tells us to make our calling and election sure. Are you convinced that God has called you into the ministry? This is very important because ministry is not a profession that we might choose. It's a calling of God. How do we know we are called? The ministry to the called is not an option, it's a necessity. As Paul expressed it, "Woe is unto me, if I preach not the gospel!" (1 Corinthians 9:16). Jeremiah decided that he wasn't going to speak anymore because it got him into so much trouble. He was thrown in jail and had his life threatened. So he decided, "Hey, I'm through. I'm out of here, man." And he said, "I will not make mention of him, nor speak any more in his name. But his word was in mine heart as a burning fire shut up in my bones, and I was weary with forbearing, and I could not stay." (Jeremiah 20:9). It takes that kind of calling because the ministry is not all glamour. There are extremely difficult times. As Peter wrote, "Beloved, think it not strange concerning the fiery trial which is to try you, as though some strange thing happened unto you:" (1 Peter 4:12). We need to understand that even if God has called you to the ministry, that calling is going to be subject to extreme testing. How certain are you that you have been called by God to serve Him?

When I first felt called to the ministry, I went to school to prepare. I had difficulty in school only because I felt I needed to get out and start the ministry. I thought, "There's the world out there dying without Jesus Christ, and here I am sitting in a classroom going through the textbook." I was sure that the world was waiting for me. So when I graduated from school and got my first assignment, you can imagine my shock when I discovered the world wasn't waiting for me. Then the testing came. It was difficult financially and it was difficult spiritually. I didn't see the fruit that I had anticipated I would see in the ministry – the immediate kinds of results and excitement.

And there were tremendous financial pressures which necessitated my taking a secular job in order to support the family and stay in the ministry. I found that I wasn't supported by the ministry. So for the first seventeen years I worked outside the church in order to support myself. Now, that was really hard because I was convinced I was called. There were times when I even questioned the call. And there were times when I asked God to change the calling. I said, "God, call me to be a businessman! I seem to do well and find ease in the business world. I find it easy to make money. And, Lord, I can be a good Christian businessman. I could support the church and support someone in the ministry." But God would not allow me to escape His call, even though there were times I endeavored to do so. The vision of serving the Lord kept burning in my heart. So it takes a sense of calling. It is so important that we each need to ask ourselves a simple question, *"Has God really called me into the ministry?"*

Hand in hand with a sense of calling comes the necessity of commitment. There are few more vital qualities a pastor can have than commitment to the Lordship of Jesus Christ. I am what I am not by my own ambitions, not by my own desires, not by my own will. I am what I am by His will. I've committed my life to Him. And if I am committed to the Lord, I will also be committed to His Word and His ministry, to serve others.

To have the right attitude in our service we need to remember the words of Jesus. He said, "...the Gentiles exercise lordship over them; and their great ones exercise authority upon them. But so shall it not be among you: but whosoever will be great among you, shall be your minister: And whosoever of you will be the chiefest, shall be servant of all." (Mark 10:42-44). It is essential to recognize that the ministry is not a place of being served, of people waiting on you, honoring you, and respecting you because you're the minister. It's actually a place of serving people, even if that means going out of your way to do it.

Recently I attended a pastors' conference and was amazed at what slobs the pastors were. They would take their coffee cups and cokes into the room where we had our meetings. Now, I had no problem with that, but when we were dismissed, they just left their coke cans and coffee cups on the floor. So I found myself going around picking up the coffee cups and coke cans, and cleaning the auditorium. I know what happens when someone comes and kicks over a coffee cup on the carpet. I didn't want to leave a bad witness of our Calvary Chapel ministers at that camp facility. So many people see the ministry as an opportunity to be served rather than to serve others. To think, "Well, someone should pick up after me because I am the minister," is not only a contradiction in terms, it's also an unbiblical attitude.

There was a time when I used to leave clothes around the house. Finally my wife said, "Look, I didn't agree to be your slave! Hang them up yourself! Why should I have to hang up your clothes?" Well, I thought about it, and she was right. I shouldn't expect her to hang up my clothes. That was an important lesson for me. I haven't been called to reign. I have been called to serve.

The night that Jesus was having the final supper with His disciples before His betrayal, arrest, and crucifixion, He took a towel and girded Himself with it. Then He went around and washed the disciple's feet. After He asked them, "Know ye what I have done to you? Ye call me Master and Lord: and ye say well; for so I am. If I then, your Lord and Master, have washed your feet; ye also ought to wash one another's feet." (John 13:12-14). As Peter said, "For even hereunto were ye called: because Christ also suffered for us, leaving us an example, that ye should follow his steps:" (1 Peter 2:21). The word "ministry" actually means service. We have been called to be servants. We are to be servants, first of our Lord, but also of His children.

It's my personal opinion that people who smoke have one of the dirtiest habits in the world. They always smell and they leave a smell wherever they go. It's so easy to detect someone who smokes. All you have to do is walk by and you can smell it on their clothes. You go into a house where people smoke, you go over and take a whiff of the drapery and it will knock you out. It's just a dirty habit. But worse than that, they throw their cigarette butts down anywhere. Then they usually take their foot and wipe it across the cigarette butt to put out the glow, leaving a mess on the sidewalk. When people come to church, many times they will come up smoking and, as they get ready to go into the church, they just throw down the cigarette, and take their foot across it. Who is supposed to pick up the cigarette butt?

As I was growing up, I was taught by my mother never to touch a cigarette butt or a cigarette. I was so averse to cigarettes that even to the present day I can't touch one without somehow feeling defiled. Every time I reach down to pick up a cigarette butt, the minute I touch it, there's something from my early childhood that just revolts. I hate it! As I walk around the church grounds and see cigarette butts, I don't like how they look on the ground, so I pick them up. But, I found that as I was picking them up I was complaining against whoever put the thing down there. I would think, "Dirty, stinking inconsiderate, careless, thoughtless people."

Then the Lord spoke to my heart. He simply said, "Who are you serving?" I said, "I am serving You, Lord." And He replied, "Then quit your griping." So don't serve with a bitter heart. Don't serve with resentment. If I'm picking up cigarette butts and thinking of dirty people, then I resent doing it. But, if I think, "Well, Lord, I'll keep Your grounds clean," then I find that I can pick them up and dispose of them without having that inner disgust because I'm doing it for Jesus—not for anyone else's approval, but just for You, Lord. As the Scriptures tell us: "Whatsoever ye do in word or deed, do all in the name of the Lord Jesus." (Colossians 3:17).

There's no more important attitude to have in the ministry. We need to serve as unto the Lord because we're going to find people obnoxious. We're going to find them unthankful. We're going to find that they're demanding, and that many times they're quite miserable to be around. So, if you think, "I've got to serve them," it will get to you. But, if you think, "I'm serving the Lord," then you'll be able to handle it. Whatever our service, we must do it as unto the Lord, knowing that from the Lord, you will receive your reward.

Don't look for the applause of men. Don't look for people to say, "Oh, thank you. Oh, you mean so much to me." For so often it won't come. I've done and done and done for people, and then have had them kick me in the teeth because I wouldn't do more. You need to keep the mental attitude of doing everything as unto the Lord, knowing that of the Lord, you will receive your reward. You've got to keep that in mind. I'm a servant of Jesus Christ. He's my Master. He's the One who will reward me for my service. I need to keep that perspective and keep the right attitude in my heart as I'm serving people. I am doing it for Him.

We must not only maintain a commitment to Jesus and to serving His people, but there must also be a commitment to the Word of God. I believe that anyone who doesn't believe that the Bible is the inspired, inerrant Word of God has no business being in the ministry. Sadly, that would probably eliminate 50% of the ministers in the United States today. Why teach from a book that you don't believe? And if you do believe that the Bible is the inspired Word of God, and that it's your duty to preach it, then, by all means, know it. Be committed to it. As Paul said to Timothy, "Study to shew thyself approved unto God, a workman that needeth not to be ashamed, rightly dividing the word of truth." (2 Timothy 2:15). You can be taught how to study the Bible, but the learning process is never ending. To the present day, I continue to commit myself to the Word of God and to studying the Word of God so as to show myself approved unto God.

CHAPTER ONE

GOD'S MODEL
FOR THE CHURCH

"Upon this rock I will build my church...."
Matt. 16:18

In Calvary Chapel we look to the book of Acts as the model for the church. We believe that church history, for the most part, has been a sad and tragic story of failure. Many horrible things have been done in the name of Jesus Christ under the banner of the church.

When I went to college I had a very difficult time because when the professors found out I was a Christian, they would start bringing up issues of church history that I was all too familiar with. My only response was, "Look, don't judge Christianity by the imperfect examples that we have seen in history. Judge it by Jesus Christ. Let's go back to what He said and what He taught. He taught, *'blessed are the merciful for they shall obtain mercy.'* Do you have a problem with that? He taught that we should love one another. Do you have a problem with that? He taught that it is more blessed to give than to receive. Do you have a problem with that?" When you talk about the basic teachings of Jesus, even skeptics have to confess that they don't have a problem. What they do have is a problem with people who have claimed to be Christians and the things they have done in the name of Christ.

In the book of Revelation, Jesus was addressing the problems of the seven churches of Asia. Even at this early date, Jesus was calling the churches to repent. He pointed out the flaws that existed, the false doctrines that had crept in, and the practices that were already sowing seeds of decay within the church. For the most part, the church had failed by the end of the first century. Gnosticism and Aryanism had begun to creep in. The development of a priesthood and the establishment of church organization started early on in the history of the church. In the book of Revelation, Jesus expressed His displeasure with all these things in His letters to the churches.

Now this was less than sixty years after the church was first founded. So it didn't take long to become so corrupt and lukewarm that the Lord was ready to spew it out of His mouth. It was nauseating to Him. As I look at church history, I don't think that things have improved. The church has only deteriorated even further. The things that the Lord spoke about to the seven churches are things that He could very well say to the church today.

So you can't look at church history and find the model for the church, just like you can't look at the history of mankind and find God's divine intention for man. Man is fallen, and so you don't see the divine ideal. The same is true of the church. You don't see the divine ideal for the church by looking at church history.

The divine ideal is found in the book of Acts. This was a church that was dynamic. It was a church led by the Holy Spirit and empowered by the Holy Spirit. It was a church that brought the Gospel to the world. Paul, writing to the Colossians some thirty years after Pentecost said, "For the hope which is laid up for you in heaven, whereof ye heard before in the word of the truth of the gospel; Which is come unto you, as it is in all the world; and bringeth forth fruit, as it doth also in you, since the day ye heard of it, and knew the grace of God in truth;" (Colossians 1:5-6). The first believers experienced a church effective in bringing the Gospel to the world.

Looking at the book of Acts, I believe we see the church as God intended it to be. The model that we find in the book of Acts is a church filled with the Holy Spirit, led by the Holy Spirit, and empowered by the Holy Spirit. It was a church where the Holy Spirit was the one directing its operation and ministry.

How dependent was the early church on the Holy Spirit? We find the Holy Spirit saying, "Separate me Barnabas and Saul for the work whereunto I have called them. And when they had fasted and prayed, and laid their hands on them, they sent them away." (Acts 13:2-3) Paul uses such phrases as, "For it seemed good to the Holy Ghost and to us." (Acts 15:28), and "they assayed to go into Bithynia: but the Spirit suffered them not." (Acts 16:7). These were men who were led by the Spirit, guided by the Spirit, and who sought the direction of the Holy Spirit.

We see in the fourth chapter of Acts how, when they were faced with heavy persecution, they prayed and sought the help and guidance of God. It was then that the Holy Spirit came upon them afresh, and they went forth speaking the Word with boldness.

There were four basic functions of the early church. Acts 2:42 tells us, "And they continued steadfastly in the apostles' doctrine and fellowship, and in breaking of bread, and in prayers." These four foundations must be instituted when developing a fellowship of believers. If we lead people to continue steadfastly in the Word of God, teaching them the apostles' doctrine, bringing them into fellowship in the body of Christ, participating in the breaking of bread, and being people of prayer, we will see God meet every other need.

The Lord certainly took care of everything for the church in Acts. "And the Lord added to the church daily, such as should be saved." (Acts 2:47). Never forget that it's not your job to add to the church. That's His job. Your job is to feed the flock, tend the flock, love the flock, and see that they're well cared for. This is especially true for a smaller flock. The Lord said, "Well done, thou good and faithful servant: thou hast been faithful over a few things, I will make thee ruler over many things: enter thou into the joy of thy lord." (Matthew 25:21). The Lord's not going to make you a ruler over many until you've been faithful with a few. Don't constantly be thinking, "Oh, but I wish we had a thousand here!" or "I wish we had five thousand here!" Minister to those eight or ten people that you do have. Be faithful in ministering to them. Be faithful in nourishing them, and the Lord will add daily, as He sees fit, those that should be saved. The size of the church is not your concern, nor should it ever be.

Now if you look at most church programs today, the chief goal is trying to add to the church. There are all these growth programs and seminars that try to show you how to add to your church. Well, it's very easy. You don't have to pay $175.00 for a seminar to find out how to grow a church. Just get the people into the Word. Get the people in prayer. Get them in fellowship and the breaking of bread, and you'll find that the Lord will add to the church daily those that should be saved.

One of the wisest things I ever did when I was still involved in a denomination was to stop counting the number of people. The church always had this chart on the wall that showed Sunday School attendance today, last Sunday, and a year ago. There was a constant emphasis on numbers. People were always being reminded of attendance statistics. *"Where are we in relationship to last Sunday?" "Where are we in relationship to a year ago?" "Where is everybody today?" "Why is it that we're down?"* The people were constantly interested in numbers. The trap of counting heads is a terrible snare to fall into. Don't do it! Just look at those that are there and realize, *"These are the ones that the Lord has brought for me to minister to today."* Give them your best, and minister to them from your heart. Minister to them diligently. As you're faithful, and as you prove yourself a faithful steward, the Lord will bring you more people to watch over, to care for, and to minister to. So be faithful to those that God has placed under your tutelage.

In the book of Acts, we see that some problems arose over a benevolence program in the church. The widows who were following the Greek culture felt they were being discriminated against, and that special favor was given to the widows who were more traditionally Jewish. So they came to the apostles with their grievances. The apostles said, "It is not desirable that we should leave the word of God and serve tables. Therefore, brethren, seek out from among you seven men of good reputation, full of the Holy Spirit and wisdom, whom we may appoint over this business; but we will give ourselves continually to prayer and to the ministry of the word." (Acts 6:3-4).

So, the Word of God was the top priority in the ministry of the early church, along with prayer. They gave themselves to the teaching of God's Word, to fellowship *(koinonia)*, to the breaking of bread, and then to prayer. "And the Lord added to the church daily, such as should be saved." (Acts 2:47). When the church is what God intends the church to be, when the church is doing what God wants the church to do, then the Lord will do what He wants to do for the church. And He will add daily to the church those that should be saved.

The kind of men that God used in the church in Acts were men who were totally surrendered to Jesus Christ, not seeking their own glory, but only seeking to bring glory unto Jesus. When the crowd assembled upon Solomon's porch, after the healing of the lame man, Peter said, "Ye men of Israel, why marvel ye at this? Or why look ye so earnestly on us, as though by our own power or holiness we had made this man to walk? The God of Abraham, and of Isaac, and of Jacob, the God of our fathers, hath glorified His Son Jesus." (Acts 3:12-13). Even Peter, after a great miracle, wouldn't take the glory or the credit. He pointed them to Jesus, to bring glory to the Lord through the miracle that was wrought.

Giving glory to God was the purpose in the early church. The men that God used were men who weren't seeking their own glory. This is something that is heavy on my own heart as we look at how men today are striving to be successful, to create a name, to bring glory unto themselves. They're always trying to position themselves so that they're in the limelight, so that the camera catches them. But Jesus insisted, the way up is down. "And whosoever shall exalt himself shall be abased; and he that shall humble himself shall be exalted." (Matthew 23:12).

So live for the kingdom of God. Seek to bring glory to Jesus Christ and the Lord will use you. It is my prayer, my constant and daily prayer, that God would keep me useable. Paul desired the same thing. He wrote to the Corinthians, "But I keep under my body, and bring it into subjection: lest that by any means, when I have preached to others, I myself should be a castaway." (1 Corinthians 9:27).

Success is a dangerous thing. If God begins to bring success to your ministry, you're in much greater danger than if you're just struggling and trying to barely make it in some little insignificant, faraway place with a fellowship of ten people. It's easy to stay on your knees in those kind of circumstances! There isn't much opportunity for you to be glorified. But when success begins to come, that's when the real danger arrives in the ministry. As people begin to look to you, it's so easy to slip into taking the credit or receiving the applause. That's the shortest path to the end of the anointing of God's Spirit. The Bible says, "For promotion cometh neither from the east, nor from the west, nor from the south. But God is the judge: He putteth down one, and setteth up another." (Psalm 75:6-7). Promotion seems to be the name of the game today. Many pastors spend all of their time and energy trying to promote a church, or trying to promote themselves. But promotion, true promotion, comes from the Lord. So be careful.

The book of Acts gives us the model for the church. It's a church that's led by the Spirit, that's teaching the Word, and that's developing oneness—that's fellowship and koinonia. It's a church that's breaking bread together and praying together. The rest is His work, and He will do it. He will add to the church daily those that should be saved.

CHURCH GOVERNMENT

"And hath put all things under his feet, and gave him to be the head over all things to the church," Eph. 1:22

We recognize that the New Testament doesn't give a clear definitive statement of God's preference for church government. In Scripture, we find three basic forms of church government. Two of them are in the New Testament, and the other one developed through church history. The first form of church government was the rule by bishops, or overseers. The Greek word is *'episkopos'*. In 1 Timothy 3:1, Paul wrote, "This is a true saying, If a man desire the office of a bishop, he desireth a good work."

Timothy gives us the qualifications for an 'episkopos.' "A bishop must be blameless, the husband of one wife, vigilant, sober, of good behaviour, given to hospitality, apt to teach; Not given to wine, no striker, not greedy of filthy lucre; but patient, not a brawler, not covetous; One that ruleth well his own house, having his children in subjection with all gravity; (For if a man know not how to rule his own house, how shall he take care of the church of God?). Not a novice, lest being lifted up with pride he fall into the condemnation of the devil. Moreover he must have a good report of them which are without; lest he fall into reproach and the snare of the devil." (1 Timothy 3:2-7).

There was another form of leadership that utilized a group of gifted men called the *'presbyteros'*, or elders. Acts 14:23 tells us, "And when they had ordained them elders (presbyteros) in every church, and had prayed with fasting, they commended them to the Lord, on whom they believed."

The New Testament clearly teaches the establishing of bishops, the *episkopos*, and the appointing of elders, the *presbyteros*. These two forms of government, by their very nature, seem to clash. Is the church to be led by the bishop, or by the board of elders? Is it the *episkopos* or the *presbyteros*? These divisions are so pronounced that today we have two denominations representing both sides of the issue. The Episcopal church follows the *episkopos*. It's a church ruled by a bishop. You also have the *presbyteros*, the Presbyterian church, ruled by a board of elders. The fact that they both exist shows that there isn't a clear definitive teaching about the correct form of church government. Both sides can present a valid case for their point of view.

Over time, a third form of church government has arisen, known as congregational rule. I don't believe that congregational rule is an option because we really never see an example in the Bible where the congregation was right. It was the congregation that was always coming and saying, "We want a king to rule over us like the other nations," making demands that were not after the will of God. I can find no Scriptural example of effective congregational rule. We do read of congregations attempting to rule. In Exodus 16:2 we read, "And the whole congregation of the children of Israel murmured against Moses and Aaron in the wilderness:" and in Numbers 14:1-3, "And all the congregation lifted up their voice, and cried; and the people wept that night. And all the children of Israel murmured against Moses and against Aaron: and the whole congregation said unto them, Would God that we had died in the land of Egypt! or would God we had died in this wilderness! And wherefore hath the LORD brought us unto this land, to fall by the sword, that our wives and our children should be a prey? were it not better for us to return into Egypt?" Moses responds to God in Numbers 14:27, "How long shall I bear with this evil congregation, which murmur against me? I have heard the murmurings of the children of Israel, which they murmur against me." So woe to the man who pastors a congregational church. Like Moses, the pastor will only find murmuring and uprisings.

These are the three basic forms of church government that we see today. The *Episkopos*, the *Presbyteros*, and the more recent Congregationalists.

Now we do find in Scripture a form of government that God established and modeled in the early history of Israel. It was a theocracy, people who were ruled by God. The nation of Israel, in its inception, was a theocratic form of government. It was God-ruled.

Their demise came when they tired of God's rule and demanded instead to have a monarchy. They said, *"We want a king to rule over us. We want to be like the other nations."* Samuel was greatly disappointed when they came to him requesting this monarchy.

Let's look at an example of theocracy in which God was ruling. Under God there was a man called Moses. Moses went to God for guidance and direction. Moses was the earthly leader who was recognized as receiving from God the guidance, direction, laws, and rules for the nation. It was recognized by the people that he was their link to God. They said, "Look we're afraid to approach Him. He's awesome. We've seen the fire and thunder. You go up and you talk to Him, and then you come down and tell us what He says, and we'll obey it. But we don't want to go. You just go." So they recognized that Moses was being directed by God. He would go up and he would receive from God and he would, in turn, come down and share it with the people.

Under Moses, the personal demands were staggering. The line of people with needs would stretch to the horizon every day. They would come to Moses for every little thing so he could judge between them and their neighbors on the issues that had arisen. "They borrowed my hoe, and they never returned it." Now this went on all day long, every day. Jethro, his father-in-law, said, "Hey, son, this is going to kill you. You can't handle this. You can't take care of the things that need to be done because of this long line of people waiting for you to give them judgment." So the Lord told Moses to take seventy of the elders of Israel and gather them into the tent of congregation. He took the Spirit that He had put upon Moses and put it upon them so that the people could come to them and they could give the rulings and judgments. If issues arose that were too difficult for them, they were then to go to Moses. Moses would then go to God to get clarification on the issue. (Exodus 18:13-27).

For additional support, Aaron and the priesthood, under Moses, oversaw the spiritual needs of the nation, like the preparation and offering of sacrifices. Under the elders and Aaron was the congregation of Israel. This is the form of government that God established for the nation of Israel.

In the church today we see this structure in a modified form. We see that Jesus Christ is the Head over the body of the church. It's His church. He's the One in charge. As pastors, we need to be like Moses, in touch with Jesus and receiving His direction and guidance. As pastors we need to be leading the church in such a way that the people know that the Lord is in control. Then, when issues come up, we can say, *"Well, let me pray about that." "Let me seek the wisdom of the Lord on this." "Let's look for the Lord's guidance."* Also, like Moses, within the church we have a Board of Elders who are there to pray with us and support us in seeking the Lord's leading for the church.

Let me warn you. First of all, you want to get elders who are men of prayer, and who recognize that God has anointed you and ordained you as the pastor of the church. Paul warned Timothy not to lay hands on any man suddenly. (1 Timothy 5:22). Really get to know the men as well as possible before giving them positions of authority. It's sort of like marriage, you really don't know your wife until you have been married to her for awhile. Many times there are a lot of surprises. It's also important to remember that problems usually arise when you start to have some success and the church begins to grow and become powerful. There are many people who have a desire for power. When they see there's money in the bank, that's when they make their move for position and control.

It's necessary to have godly men who recognize that God has called and ordained you as the pastor of the church. Men who will work with you and support those things that God is directing you, as the pastor, to implement within the church. A good Board is one of the greatest assets that you can have in your ministry. I thank God that here at Calvary Chapel Costa Mesa we have been blessed with great men of God serving on the Board. We usually look at the Saturday night prayer meetings or at the all-night prayer watch for men to serve on the Board. We want men of prayer. We want men who are seeking God and the will of God. We are blessed with such men on our Board, and I thank God for them.

Now, real elders aren't a bunch of *"yes"* men, but they are men yielded to the Holy Spirit. They're a real buffer and protection for me. Their job is to interface with the congregation. The congregation brings any problems that they see to them. Many times they will simply reply, "Well, this is the church policy, and this is why we do things in this way." And it doesn't go any further. Sometimes at the Board Meeting they will bring a list of questions such as, "Well this has been brought before me. How do you feel about this?" On occasion I'll answer, "Well, I don't have any real feelings. Let's seek the Lord." But in many instances I will just let them work out the issues.

When I was a very young pastor in Tucson, Arizona (the second church that I pastored), we had an annual Fourth of July picnic at Mt. Lemon. Now Tucson on the Fourth of July, is 110 degrees in the valley, so we would go up to Mt. Lemon where the temperatures are cooler. The state park on Mt. Lemon had a great area for picnics. They had restrooms, running water, tables and playgrounds. It was a wonderful place for the church to go and have our Fourth of July picnic. And it was a good time for fellowship. Before one Fourth of July one of our members said, "I have an acre of ground up on Mt. Lemon. And rather than mixing with the worldly crowd in the state park, I think that it would be great if the church would come up and have the picnic on my acre of ground." We said, "Do you have any water?" And he said "No." "Do you have any restrooms?" "No, just an acre of ground." It was also another five miles up the road from the state park to his acre. He countered with, "But it would be great to have a day of fasting and prayer." Now how can anyone, as a pastor, speak against fasting and prayer without appearing really unspiritual before the people?

So a group of people in the church discussed it, and they agreed it would be wonderful to have a day of fasting and prayer up there on the acre of ground. It would be just us, and we'd have a glorious time.

There was another group of people in the church who said, "We're not going to take our kids up to a place where we don't have water. And who is going to watch the kids, and what are they going to do while we're fasting and praying? There are no restrooms. If you go up there we aren't going." Now the spiritual group said, "Well, if you go to the state park, we're not going." They were manifesting real spirituality. There was a very sharp division in the congregation.

Here our whole Fourth of July picnic, that had been such a glorious delight year after year, was going to be scuttled because of this division. Both sides came to me and said, "Chuck, where are we going to have the Fourth of July picnic?" So with wisdom from the Lord beyond my years, I said, "We will let the Board decide that." We had a Board Meeting and it was unanimously decided to go to the state park. I went back to the people and said, "The Board has decided that we should have the picnic at the state park." I was then able to go to the spiritual ones who wanted to fast and pray and say, "That's a great idea. It would be wonderful to spend a day fasting and praying. Maybe we can go some other time, just us, and fast and pray. But as far as the picnic goes they felt it best to go to the state park."

Because the Board made the decision, I was free to minister to both sides. The Board became the buffer. And it's great to have a buffer like that because then people don't polarize against you saying, "It was the pastor who decided, and I don't agree with his decision." The Board decided, and they became a buffer for me.

I believe that God's model is that the pastor is ruled over by the Lord and recognized by the congregation as God's anointed instrument to lead the

church, with the Board guiding and directing.
Complementing this is the role of the assisting pastors.
They are there to minister to the spiritual needs of the
people on a daily basis. With these components in
place, there is a great form of church government
where you, as the pastor, are not in the position of a
hireling. Becoming a hireling is a real danger when the
church is run by a Presbyterian kind of a government,
and the Board is ruling over the church. The pastor is
hired by the Board and can be fired by the Board in the
same fashion. With that kind of rule the pastor
becomes a hireling.

The same is true with congregational rule. A pastor
is hired by the congregation, rather than ordained by
the Lord who is the Head of the body. He's not
appointed by Jesus Christ, the Head of the body, but
instead he's elected or selected by the Board or by the
congregation. Here again, the pastor becomes a
hireling. I don't believe that anyone can do his best
work as a hireling.

It is my belief that everyone should be a deacon.
The ministry of helps was the essence of the deacon's
function. They were to look after the facilities. They
were to look after the needs of the congregation and
help the sick. One of the worst things to do is to start
giving titles to people in the church, especially a title
that distinguishes one above another. That's a
dangerous thing.

A word concerning the spiritual qualifications for
church leadership: Jude said in his benediction, "Now
unto him that is able to keep you from falling, and to
present you faultless before the presence of his glory
with exceeding joy," (Jude 1:24). I am only blameless
as I am in Christ Jesus. Still, it's true that we've all
sinned and fall short of the glory of God. If anybody
realized his disqualification for the ministry, it was
Paul, the apostle, who said, "Unto me, who am less

than the least of all saints, is this grace given, that I should preach among the Gentiles the unsearchable riches of Christ;" (Ephesians 3:8). He was saying, "I'm less than the least of all of the saints. I'm not really worthy to be called an apostle because I persecuted the church of God." He refers to himself elsewhere saying, "This grace is given to the chiefest of sinners." Paul realized that his position was given only by the grace of God. As he said in 1 Corinthians 15:10, "By the grace of God I am what I am." He truly recognized that in Christ he was blameless. So the key qualification for a pastor or leader in the church is to be "in Christ Jesus" and, in this state, blameless.

I believe that if a man is not abiding in Christ, but walking in the flesh, he is disqualified from the position of an 'episkopos.' Walking in the flesh describes a practiced lifestyle. Satan is out to destroy anyone with an effective ministry and I believe that all of us are capable of stumbling. As Jesus said to Peter, "And the Lord said, Simon, Simon, behold, Satan hath desired to have you, that he may sift you as wheat: But I have prayed for thee, that thy faith fail not: and when thou art converted, strengthen thy brethren." (Luke 22:31-32).

Peter responded, "Though all men shall be offended because of thee, yet will I never be offended." (Matthew 26:33). He was saying, "Lord, though they all may forsake you, I would never forsake! Lord, I would die for you!" That self-confidence had to be dealt with before he could realize his total dependency upon the Holy Spirit. It was something that had to be dealt with in his life. And I think it's something that has to be dealt with in all our lives. When we have areas of self-confidence, the Lord gradually shows us that, in and of ourselves, we can do nothing. As Paul said, "For I know that in me (that is, in my flesh,) dwelleth no good thing:" (Romans 7:18). So whenever we think that we are the exceptions to the rule, the Lord allows us to stumble, to teach us our total reliance upon Him.

When we step into the flesh and decide that we're going to live after the flesh, we disqualify ourselves from our positions of service. But if we take the word *'blameless'* in a very literal sense, then all of us might as well pack up and go get a job selling cars. I believe that repentance is the key, true repentance, and once there's true repentance, then there is forgiveness, and restoration can begin. But there has to be true repentance, a real turning away from sin.

I've observed that those churches that follow the rule of the Eldership so often are not really looking for a pastor as much as they're looking for a hireling. Their idea of a pastor is, *"Someone who is going to come in and dance to our beat. We'll pull the strings and as long as you respond and react, you're a fair-haired employee. But if you dare to want to step out on your own, then it's a different story."*

Before we came to Calvary Chapel, I had started an independent church in Corona that was an outgrowth of a home Bible study. Some of the men involved in the home Bible study decided to form a corporation which they called *"Corona Christian Association"*. They set up the corporation so that people could tithe into it and start building up funds, primarily to put me on the radio in Corona. These men who set up the corporation were the corporate officers. So we started a radio broadcast that immediately brought in a multitude of people.

I had been wanting to leave the denomination I was involved in and become independent. These men invited me to start a church in Corona, which I did. We began the Corona Christian Center. It was blessed of God. I was still living in Newport Beach and driving there on Sunday. We'd spend the day there and then we'd come home Sunday night. One Sunday afternoon when my family was there with me at the American Legion hall that we rented, I decided to put the chairs in a circle, rather than in rows. I removed the pulpit and just set up a big circle of chairs. As the people came in that night we all sat in a circle, like in the home Bible studies. Rather than singing three hymns out of the hymnal, accompanied by the organ and the piano, we just sang. I led them a cappella in worship choruses. After that we had prayer time, what we called 'directed prayer', where we would bring up an issue and people in the circle would pray. Then I taught, just sitting there in the chair, in an informal way.

I felt that it was led by the Spirit and was very dynamic. I mean it was exciting! There were fellows that night who led out in prayer who had never prayed publicly in their lives. So many of them were really touched and moved. However, the Board Members got together afterward for a special Board Meeting. They called me the next morning and wanted to know just what I thought I was doing, and they let me know that they didn't want me to do that again. At the time I thought, "Well, I thought this might be my life's ministry. But it won't be. I'm not going to be under these kinds of restrictions. I must be open to be led by the Spirit."

So when we came to Calvary Chapel and established the bylaws, we didn't create a Presbyterian form of government. It was more of an *Episkopos* form of government for Calvary Chapel. We believe that God's model is that the pastor is ruled by the Lord and aided by the Elders to discover the mind and will of Jesus Christ for His church. This in turn is implemented by the Assistant Pastors.

CHAPTER THREE

EMPOWERED BY THE SPIRIT

*"But ye shall receive power, after that the Holy
Ghost is come upon you: and ye shall be witnesses
unto me both in Jerusalem, and in all Judaea, and
in Samaria, and unto the uttermost part of the
earth."*
Acts 1:8

Another Calvary Chapel distinctive is our position
concerning the Holy Spirit. We believe that there is an
experience of the empowering of the Holy Spirit in the
life of a believer that is distinct and separate from the
indwelling of the Spirit that takes place at conversion.
Paul asked the Ephesians if they received the Holy
Spirit when they believed, or since they believed. No
matter which translation you choose, the Scriptures
clearly teach that there is an experience with the Holy
Spirit that is separate and distinct from that of
salvation.

When Philip went to Samaria preaching Christ
unto them, many believed and were baptized. When
the church in Jerusalem heard that the Samaritans
had received the Gospel, they sent Peter and John,

"Who, when they were come down, prayed for them, that they might receive the Holy Ghost: (For as yet he was fallen upon none of them: only they were baptized in the name of the Lord Jesus.)" (Acts 8:15-16). Once again we see an experience of the Holy Spirit that was separate and distinct from conversion.

In the second chapter of Acts, when the people said, "Men and brethren, what shall we do? Then Peter said unto them, Repent, and be baptized every one of you in the name of Jesus Christ for the remission of sins, and ye shall receive the gift of the Holy Ghost." (Acts 2:37-38). Paul was converted on the road to Damascus, but Ananias came to him and laid hands on him that he might receive his sight and receive the Holy Spirit. (Acts 9).

We believe there is an empowering experience with the Holy Spirit that is separate and distinct from conversion. We acknowledge a three-fold relationship between the Holy Spirit and the believer that is represented by three Greek prepositions—'para', 'en', and 'epi.'

In John 14, Jesus told the disciples, "And I will pray the Father, and he shall give you another Comforter, that he may abide with you for ever; Even the Spirit of truth; whom the world cannot receive, because it seeth him not, neither knoweth him: but ye know him; for he dwelleth with you, and shall be in you." (John 14:16-17). *'With you'* speaks of the *'para'* relationship, the coming alongside. The *'en'* in the phrase *'in you'* is equivalent to our English preposition *'in'* as in *"He is going to dwell in you."*

We believe that the Holy Spirit is dwelling <u>with</u> a person prior to conversion. He is the One convicting him of his sin, convincing him that Jesus Christ is the only answer. The Holy Spirit is constantly testifying of sin, of righteousness, and of judgment to come. We also believe that the moment a person receives the witness of the Holy Spirit, Jesus takes away his sin. When anyone invites Jesus to come into his heart, to take over the rule and control of his life, we believe that the Holy Spirit then comes into that person's life. He is with each one of us to bring us to Christ, and when we come to Christ, He begins then to dwell in us.

Paul said, "...know ye not that your body is the temple of the Holy Ghost which is in you, which ye have of God, and ye are not your own? For you are bought with a price;" (1 Corinthians 6:19-20). He also told the Ephesians, "And be not drunk with wine, wherein is excess; but be filled with the Spirit;" (Ephesians 5:18). Thus, we believe that every born again believing child of God has the Holy Spirit dwelling in him. He is under the injunction of the Scriptures to yield his body to the control of the Holy Spirit and to be constantly filled with the Holy Spirit.

We also believe that the Holy Spirit provides the power in the life of the believer to give him victory over sin and over the flesh. We are taught to walk after the Spirit and not after the flesh. He that walks after the Spirit will not fulfill the lusts of the flesh. The Holy Spirit is the power over the flesh life, giving us power over our fallen nature. He is the power in our life to conform us into the image of Jesus Christ. "But we all, with open face beholding as in a glass the glory of the Lord, are changed into the same image from glory to glory, even as by the Spirit of the Lord." (2 Corinthians 3:18). So we see the dynamic power of the Spirit in us which comes when we accept Jesus. He begins that work in us of transforming us into the image of Jesus Christ.

We believe that there is a third relationship that the believer can have that is separate and distinct from the first two. In Acts 1:8 we see this promise, "But ye shall receive power, after that the Holy Ghost is come upon you." This relationship is when the Holy Spirit comes <u>upon</u> you. The word is *'epi'* in the Greek, which means *'upon'* or *'over.'* I prefer the translation of *'overflow'* because I believe that this experience allows the Holy Spirit to flow forth out of our lives. Our lives then are not just a vessel containing the Spirit, but they become channels by which the Spirit flows forth to touch the world around us. I also believe that this is the objective work of the Spirit. The first work is subjective, when the changes and the transformations take place within me. This *'coming upon'* experience provides objective evidence of the dynamic power of the Holy Spirit, allowing us to be effective witnesses for Jesus Christ. That is God's ideal and plan, that my life be the instrument through which He can reach the world around me as the Spirit flows forth, as the dynamic of the Spirit goes forth out of my life.

We find in the New Testament that Jesus breathed on His disciples and said, "Receive ye the Holy Spirit." (John 20:22). I believe that when Jesus breathed on them and said, "Receive ye the Holy Spirit," that they received the Holy Spirit.

Some people claim, "Well, that was just a symbolic action." Show me the Scripture where we are told that this was just symbolic! Why didn't John say, "Well, He did a symbolic thing here." There's no Scriptural support to say that this was only a symbolic action. I believe that at that moment the disciples were born again by the Spirit of God.

Then Jesus told His disciples that they were to wait in Jerusalem until they received the promise of the Father which He had been talking to them about. "For John truly baptized with water; but ye shall be baptized with the Holy Ghost not many days hence." (Acts 1:5). He also said, "But ye shall receive power (dunamis), after that the Holy Ghost is come upon (epi) you," (Acts 1:8). They needed that overflowing of the Spirit to effectively serve the Lord.

We believe that this is the experience that Jesus was referring to in John 7 when, on the great day of the Feast of Tabernacles, He stood and cried to the assembled multitude, "If any man thirst, let him come unto me, and drink. He that believeth on me, as the scripture hath said, out of his belly shall flow rivers of living water." (John 7:37-38). And John, giving the commentary, wrote, "(But this spake he of the Spirit, which they that believe on him should receive: for the Holy Ghost was not yet given; because that Jesus was not yet glorified.)" (John 7:39). This 'coming upon' has been referred to as the baptism of the Holy Spirit, or the overflow of the Spirit. What kind of overflow would that be? It would be like a torrent of living water flowing out of the life of the believer.

So it's one thing to be filled with the Spirit, and it's quite another to have the Spirit flowing out. The inlet of the Spirit is powerful and dynamic, but there has to be that flowing forth of the Spirit from my life to affect and touch others around me.

Jesus made three promises to us about the Spirit—He is with you, He shall be in you, and you will receive the power when He comes over you, or upon you. The Holy Spirit is <u>with</u> us prior to conversion. It's the Holy Spirit that reproves the world of sin, of righteousness, and of judgment. It's the Holy Spirit who brings conviction of sin to your heart. It's the Holy Spirit that draws you to Jesus Christ and points out that Jesus is the only answer to your sin. It's the Holy Spirit who, once having drawn you to Christ, when you open the door, comes into your life and begins to indwell you. The power of the Holy Spirit indwelling you conforms your character into the image of Jesus Christ. The Holy Spirit helps you to live the Christian life and conforms you into His image. He does for you what you can't do for yourself.

As Paul said, "But we all, with open face beholding as in a glass the glory of the Lord, are changed into the same image from glory to glory, even as by the Spirit of the Lord." (2 Corinthians 3:18). He also said, "What? know ye not that your body is the temple of the Holy Ghost which is in you, which ye have of God, and ye are not your own? For ye are bought with a price: therefore glorify God in your body, and in your spirit, which are God's." (1 Corinthians 6:19-20). Through God's work of salvation my body has become the temple of the Spirit. He's dwelling in me. He has the power to change me in order to conform me into the image of Jesus Christ.

It's the Lord's desire that He flow forth out of my life. It's one thing to pour water into a cup, but it's another thing to pour it out of the cup. It's one thing to have the Holy Spirit poured into your life and another thing to allow the Holy Spirit to pour out of your life. That's the necessary dynamic for the ministry. Even the disciples were not permitted to engage in the ministry until they had received this dynamic of the Spirit. "Being assembled together with them, commanded them that they should not depart from Jerusalem, but wait for the promise of the Father, which, saith he, ye have heard of me." (Acts 1:4). The "promise of the Father" is this dynamic of the Holy Spirit. It's the 'epi' experience, the coming upon.

This experience is usually separate from salvation, but it can be concurrent with salvation, like in the case of the house of Cornelius. As Peter was speaking, the Holy Spirit came upon them, 'epi', and they began to speak in tongues. So the apostles decided that if God would baptize them with the Spirit, the apostles should also allow them to be baptized with water. (Acts 10).

So we believe that there is an experience with the Holy Spirit that is distinct from conversion and indwelling. Some call it baptism. Some call it being filled with the Spirit. Whatever we choose to call it, it means being overflowed with the Spirit. You can fill a cup, but if you keep pouring, it's going to overflow. This is distinct from just being filled. This is overflowing with the Spirit. Some call it the gift of the Spirit. Some call it the empowering of the Spirit. It doesn't matter what you call it, the main thing is that you have it. We could argue over theological terms, but the experience is described as a gushing forth of torrents of living water from our innermost being. So whatever name you call it isn't important. The main question we must ask concerning this necessary empowering experience for the ministry is simple: **DO YOU HAVE IT?**

Chapter Four

Building The Church
God's Way

*"Not by might, nor by power, but by my spirit,
saith the LORD of hosts."*
Zech. 4:6

Another distinctive characteristic of Calvary
Chapel is our relaxed casual style. We don't get
involved in a lot of spiritual hype. We don't try to
motivate people carnally, and we aren't apt to shout at
the congregation. I believe this stems from our belief
and trust in Jesus Christ and in the Holy Spirit. We
are of the belief that *if the Lord doesn't build the house,
they labor in vain who build it,* so all of our hype and
pressure aren't really going to do the job. We simply
trust in the work of the Holy Spirit, and of Jesus
Christ who is building His church as He said He
would.

If we have complete confidence that it's His church,
that He's going to build it, and that He's going to do
His job, then all I have to do is be faithful. I simply
need to watch His work, and then the pressure isn't on

me. I don't get all hyped or pressured because the work of God isn't my responsibility. It's not my church. It's His church. I believe that it's very important to remember this, because if you try to carry the load and bear the burden, you'll find that it's too great for you. You'll find yourself under pressure to create schemes and hypes, and then you begin to push and manipulate people. That isn't the Calvary Chapel style.

Back in 1969, we purchased an acre and a half of land just a block from our current site, on the corner of Sunflower and Greenville. There was an old country school there. We dismantled it and used the materials to build our little chapel. Because we used the existing materials, we were able to build the chapel for $40,000.00, including the pews. After two years the chapel was totally inadequate. We were into triple services, setting up five hundred chairs in the patio, and people were parking all the way up past the Los Angeles Times building up to the freeway on Fairview. So we knew that we had to do something.

At that time, the parcel of property that Calvary Chapel occupies today came up for sale. One of the fellows in the church was a Realtor. He had put together a group that bought this 11-acre property, planning to turn it for a profit. They were speculating on it and had several deals pending, but the city of Santa Ana rejected all of the proposed uses. They had a balloon payment of $350,000 coming due on the property and weren't in a position to pay it. They had actually stopped making the monthly interest payments to the lady who owned the property, and finally lost it.

The Realtor who was involved in our fellowship came to me and suggested that the church obtain the property. My response was, "Well, what in the world will we ever do with eleven acres?" He suggested that we could always sell off half of it. Then another fellow in the church came to me and said he was certain we could get the land for $300,000.00. I said, "Ridiculous! There's no way she'd sell it for $300,000.00 because she just foreclosed on a note for $350,000.00. Why would she sell it to us for $300,000.00?" Then he said, "Well, I happen to know a few things about the lady's situation. She had been paying the taxes with the interest payments that these guys were giving her. Because they hadn't made any payments, she didn't really have the money to pay the taxes. She's close to eighty, she needs the cash, and I think that if we made a $300,000.00 cash offer, she would take it."

I said, "That sounds great, but where in the world will we get $300,000.00 cash?" He replied, "If we can buy it for $300,000.00 then you can borrow half that amount from the savings and loan. They'll loan fifty percent on property, we have $110,000.00 in the bank, and I'll loan the $90,000.00 interest free, for a year." So I said, "Well, she'll never take it." Then he said, "Will you give me the permission to offer it to her in the name of the church?" "Sure," I replied. A short time later he called me up and said, "Well, Chuck, she's accepted." My first thought was, "Well, great! But what do I do now?"

At that time Fairview Street had just been completed through to Sunflower. I used to drive up to the corner of Fairview and Sunflower on my way from the other chapel. As I waited for the green arrow to turn left, I'd look over at this big huge field, and begin to panic. I thought, "You know, God has been good to us. We've paid off all of the debts, and we don't owe anything. We have $60,000.00 in the bank, we're running a surplus, and things are going so well. What am I doing to this flock of people, putting them into debt along with the potential of having to build on this? What am I doing? Where is my head?"

I would go into a cold sweat trying to figure the thing out. Then the Lord would speak to my heart and say, "Whose church is it?" I'd answer, "Well, it's your church." Then He'd reply, "Well, then, why are you worrying about bankruptcy?" I thought, "Why am I? I'm not the one going bankrupt. The Lord will be the One bankrupt, so why should I worry? Then He would say, "Who created the problem?" And I'd answer, "You did. You're the One that's brought all the people. You created this problem of needing more space." So He assured me that it was His church and His problem. He created the situation. Then I would get relief, until the next time I pulled up to the corner and looked at the property. I'm sort of hardheaded, so this was a process that continued for a period of time.

Realizing that our fellowship was His church relieved me from the burden. I didn't have to carry the load myself, and I could stay relaxed. It was His church so He would take care of it. Jesus said, "Upon this rock I will build my church." (Matthew 16:18). He didn't say, "Upon this rock you will build my church." We need to realize that it's His church and He's the One who said He would build it. When Jesus asked Peter the question, "Lovest thou me?" (John 21:16), Peter answered , "Yea, Lord; thou knowest that I love thee". Jesus then didn't say, "Go out and build my church." He said, "Feed my sheep"—that is, "tend them and take care of them." It's His job to add to the church, His job to build the church. My job is just to love the sheep, take care of them, watch over them, feed them, tend them, and trust the Lord to build the church and add those that should be saved.

We've discovered that whenever you strive to gain, you must then strive to maintain what you've gained. If you really pushed and pressured to gain it, you have the pressure to keep it going. Maintenance is tough if it's a man-made, man-built program.

A long time ago, I was in a denomination and was under pressure to build the church. I was using every kind of device suggested and offered. There were church growth programs and various kinds of contests. I tried them all in an effort to build the church. I discovered firsthand that when you strive to gain, then you must strive to maintain. When you don't strive to gain, you don't have to strive to maintain. If it's the Lord's work, if He's done it, and He's added, then you don't have to strive to keep the thing going. It's that striving to maintain that creates ministerial burnout. It's the thing that'll kill you. It's the thing that'll run you into the ground. It's the thing that will lead you into all kinds of aberrant practices. Because you've striven to gain this crowd, you've now got a crowd that you must strive to hold, and that can be really tough.

Throughout the country we see many large churches that have resulted from tremendous growth programs. But you have to keep that program going. You have to keep it oiled and greased and moving, or the thing begins to fall. Then, all of the striving and all of the hype that it takes to maintain the program will absolutely kill you. There are a lot of super churches today, but there are also a lot of tired leaders, because of their striving to maintain what they've built.

Striving to gain doesn't just mean buying into the latest church growth program to come down the line. It can also happen in a hyped-up spiritual environment, where church growth is created by spiritual and emotional excitement and the hyping of the gifts of the Spirit. Again you've got a very difficult kind of situation, because if you use this spiritual hype to attract and draw your crowd, you've started down a one-way street that only gets more difficult as you go. You see, if you appeal to people through the supernatural and spectacular, and if that's your big forte, then you have to continue to get other, more exotic spiritual experiences to hold the crowd that you have drawn through these kinds of phenomena.

There is something about our human nature that, no matter how appealing or exotic an experience might be, we soon tire of it and want something else—a new twist, a new angle, a new attraction to power. It seems like it takes more and more power to maintain the same level of excitement and thrill.

A case in point: my boating experience began years ago with a little 12-footer and a Johnson 25hp engine. That was exciting. We learned to ski. Someone had to sit out on the end of the hull to keep the nose down to get the skier up, but we learned to ski with it. It was wonderful for the first summer. During the winter we bought a Javelin hull, fiber glassed it, and fixed it up. It was a 14-footer with a great hull! But then the little Johnson 25hp wouldn't do for the Javelin hull, so we got a Mercury 55E, and that was much better. Nobody had to get out on the front to get the skier up. That was great! But, by the end of the summer there were boats passing us, so we traded in the Mercury 55E for a Mercury 75E. But then the 14-foot Javelin hull wasn't quite nice enough for the Mercury 75E. I thought, "Well, outboards are o.k., but you really need to go to an inboard motor," so we got a Chevy 354. When do you stop? Fortunately, I did stop, but there's always something more. It was just a little bit bigger, a little bit nicer.

It's the same with the attraction generated by spiritual hype. You can only hear so many *"Thus saith the Lord's"* before they don't have the same impact or rush anymore. So you have to keep doing something new, something different. You'll ultimately get to the place where you're laughing uncontrollably or barking like a dog or roaring like a lion. Look how some churches have gone from one bizarre practice to another, to another, and to another. It's an insatiable kind of thing. You run out of the legitimate, and you begin to revert to the illegitimate. You have to keep fanning that lust for novel, bizarre, and different kinds of experiences that will continue to give the same kind of a spiritual rush that people have come to desire and long for.

Calvary Chapels are minus the hype. We're not into the carnal pursuit of new programs or spiritual hype to try to appeal to people. It's the Word of God that we trust in, that we teach, that we rely on. It's the foundation upon which we are built. It's inexhaustible. There's no burnout with it. It just keeps going on and on and on.

For this reason, we have a relaxed, casual style that's reflected in our ministry. It's His church so we don't have to sweat it. We're not really into seminars on how to build a church, how to create a user-friendly church, or how to develop a five-year plan. Who knows if we'll even be here five years from now! Let's minister for today!

I was asked to speak at a leadership seminar in Phoenix to a group of social strategists who study various social trends and develop plans for the church as we enter the new millennium. Some pretty prominent fellows were on this panel discussing strategies. "How are we going to meet the needs for the future and develop the appropriate church strategies?"

Well, I upset the moderator because I said, "I have this philosophy, 'If it isn't broken, don't fix it.' God continues to bless the teaching of His Word, the church continues to grow, the Lord continues to add daily, and He honors His Word like He said He would. I'm satisfied that as long as God is blessing the Word, I will keep teaching the Word. Why should I change? Why should I try to remodel it when it's still working? If the day should come when it doesn't work anymore, then the Word of God has failed, so why even teach it?"

Of course, the moderator became very upset with that, and the rest of the day we were trading barbs back and forth. Interestingly enough, I've never been asked to speak again at those wonderful conferences.

I find that by the time I get through with the Old Testament, I am hungry and ready to get into the New Testament. By the time I am finished with the New Testament it's exciting to get back to Genesis in the Old Testament. It keeps building every time you go through it. You gain and learn so much more. You've been enriched, and so have the people. It never gets old. It never gets stale. It never gets to the place where you have to find some new kind of gimmick or angle or experience. It's just the Word of God, which is alive and powerful and ministers to the spirit of people.

CHAPTER FIVE

GRACE UPON GRACE

"For it is a good thing that the heart be established with grace..."
Heb. 13:9

Calvary Chapel has a distinctive position on the subject of God's grace. We realize that without the grace of God none of us would have a chance. We need the grace of God in our lives. We need it daily. We experience it, and we're saved by it personally. But we also stand in grace. We believe in the love and grace that seeks to restore the fallen.

There are some churches that are severely lacking in the grace of God. There's often a very harsh, inflexible, and severe form of legalism that allows no room for repentance and restoration. You would be amazed at the flack that I've taken because I want to help restore those who are fallen. Whenever I see a talented servant of God fall to the lures of the enemy, I get angry with Satan who seeks to rip off some of our finest servants.

We have taken a very strong position on grace. We believe that the Bible does teach that God is gracious. That's one of His chief characteristics in dealing with man. If He wasn't a God of grace, none of us would stand a chance! We all need the grace and the mercy of God. Whenever I pray, I never ask God for justice, unless I'm praying about somebody else. Whenever I'm praying about myself, it's always, "Grace!" or, "Mercy, Lord, mercy! Have mercy on me! Deal with justice with that guy that's wronged me, but, Lord, I want mercy."

It's interesting that, having received mercy, having received grace, the Lord emphasizes our need to show mercy and to show grace. He said, "Blessed are the merciful: for they shall obtain mercy." (Matthew 5:7).

It's interesting that Jesus seems to equate forgiveness with our being willing to forgive. This is evident in what we commonly refer to as The Lord's Prayer. At the end of that model prayer, He emphasizes only one of the petitions, the request we make concerning forgiveness. "But if ye forgive not men their trespasses, neither will your Father forgive your trespasses." (Matthew 6:15).

Jesus gave parables that dealt with the necessity of forgiveness. In Matthew 18, we see the master who forgave his servant's sixteen-million dollar debt. But that servant went out to a fellow servant that owed him only sixteen dollars and had him thrown in debtor's prison. The master then called the first servant, and said, "How much did you owe me? And did I not forgive you? How is it that I heard that you've had this fellow servant in prison for his debt?" He rebuked him, and he ordered him to be cast into prison, until he had paid the uttermost farthing." (Matthew 18:23-35).

If we've been forgiven so much, surely we should forgive! Having received the grace of God, we should manifest that grace of God to those who have fallen. I need the grace of God daily. I stand in the grace of God. I've been saved by grace, not because of works, so that the glory goes to God for what He has done. I can't boast in what I've done. I've done nothing. It isn't by works of righteousness, but by His grace, that we are saved.

This is a theme we find throughout the New Testament, and therefore it's a theme we emphasize. The books of Romans and Galatians become very significant because they both set forth the grace of God and righteousness through faith. This is in direct contrast with the self-righteousness that one attains through the works of the law.

We believe in seeking to restore those who have fallen, as Paul taught to the Galatians, "Brethren, if a man be overtaken in a fault, ye which are spiritual, restore such an one in the spirit of meekness; considering thyself, lest thou also be tempted." (Galatians 6:1). I thank the Lord for the grace that I've received, and having received God's grace, I seek to extend it to others.

I get angry at Satan when I hear of a gifted minister who has fallen. Those that have great abilities and great talents for the Lord seem to be a special target of Satan. I'm just not willing to let Satan have a victory. I try to reclaim these men for the kingdom of God so that they might use their talents for the Lord.

I've done a lot of restoration in my life. It's just something that I love to do. I love to take old wrecks and make something attractive out of them. I've got a 1957 Ford Skyliner. Now, if you had seen it when I first got it, it looked like it was ready for the junk yard. But what fulfillment there is in taking something like that, taking time and working with it, pulling it apart and sanding it, getting the rust out, repainting it, and putting it back together, then finally seeing something beautiful and attractive made out of something that was just a wreck. There's a joy and a fulfillment in it. I also love to do that with old houses. My daughter always buys fixer-uppers, and then says, "Daddy, come over." I love to take these old fixer-uppers, remodel them, and make something attractive, modern, and beautiful out of them. And the same holds true with lives that Satan has really fouled up.

I love to take, develop, remold, and rebuild lives that were a real wreck. Look at most of the Calvary Chapel ministers! Their lives were a real wreck. But look at how God has restored, and look at the wealth and the value that have come out of these lives. It's a beautiful work of God today, to see what the world has cast off and viewed as hopeless wrecks be transformed into glorious vessels of honor.

We believe that having been forgiven, we need to be forgiving. Having received mercy, we must show mercy. Having received grace, we must be graceful. Showing and extending God's grace is an important part of the Calvary Chapel ministry.

In John's Gospel, in chapter eight, we have a very interesting story. Jesus had come into the temple, and in verse two He sat down to teach. Suddenly, His teaching was interrupted by a commotion. There was hysterical sobbing and crying. "And the scribes and Pharisees brought unto him a woman taken in adultery; and when they had set her in the midst, They say unto him, Master, this woman was taken in adultery, in the very act." (John 8:3-4).

The enemies of Christ were constantly trying to put His teaching at odds with Moses. People, in general, recognized that Moses was the instrument who brought them the law of God. There was no question about Moses' authority. He spoke for God.

If Jesus said something that was contrary to the law of Moses, then Jesus couldn't claim to be of God. That was the whole issue on divorce. They questioned Jesus about whether a man could put away his wife for any cause. Jesus answered, "And I say unto you, Whosoever shall put away his wife, except it be for fornication, and shall marry another, committeth adultery: and whoso marrieth her which is put away doth commit adultery." (Matthew 19:9). They responded by saying that Moses said they could divorce by just writing a bill of divorcement. They thought they had trapped Jesus. Jesus then went back before Moses and said that in the beginning it wasn't so. Moses, because of the hardness of the people's hearts, gave the woman a writing of a bill of divorcement, but in the beginning it was not so.

So, here again they were seeking to pit Him against the Mosaic Law. "Now Moses in the law commanded us, that such should be stoned: but what sayest thou? This they said, tempting him, that they might have to accuse him." (John 8:5-6). This was very obvious. But Jesus didn't say anything. He just stooped down and with His finger wrote on the ground as if He didn't even hear them.

Now what did He write on the ground? I don't really know. Maybe he wrote, "Where is the man?" They had said, "We caught her in the very act." Well, they couldn't catch her in the act without catching the man too. According to Moses' law they were both to be stoned. So if they were really interested in keeping the Mosaic Law, they would have been dragging the guy there, too. Maybe the guy was a friend and they let him go. This wasn't really justice.

Jesus' enemies were upset. He was just writing on the ground as though He was ignoring them. So they pressed the question. Finally, He stood up and said to them, "He that is without sin among you, let him first cast a stone at her." (John 8:7). Again He stooped down and wrote on the ground. This time I think I know what He wrote. He very well may have written the names of the men that were standing there ready to condemn, probably starting with the oldest. I think He began to write a lot of sins that the oldest man had been committing, maybe a girlfriend that he had, and Jesus started detailing some of the activities that they had been engaged in. Then finally this man said, "Oh, I remember my wife told me to get home early today, fellows. I have to go." After he took off, Jesus wrote down the name of the next oldest, and began to write down a few things that he had been doing until that man took off. One by one this continued, from the oldest to the youngest, until finally there was no one left. Jesus then stood up, and looking at the woman, said to her, "Woman, where are those thine accusers? hath no man condemned thee?" She said, "No man, Lord." Then Jesus said to her, "Neither do I condemn thee: go, and sin no more." (John 8:10-11).

What a beautiful response of Jesus. "Neither do I condemn you; go your way, and sin no more."

When there's a serious accident and cars are banged up and people's bodies are battered, cut, bleeding, and lying there in the street, there are two types of emergency vehicles that arrive on the scene. The first to arrive is usually the police, and their job is to develop a safety zone to control the traffic. Then they get out their pads and look at the positions of the cars. They measure the skid marks and start interviewing witnesses.

Their job is to find out who violated the law. Who's to blame for this tragedy? Their chief concern is to determine what laws were violated and who is at fault for what happened.

The second type of vehicle contains the paramedics. They could care less who is to blame. There are people bleeding in the street. Their job is to minister to those bleeding people, check the heart monitor, put bandages on them, look to see if there are broken bones, get them on the stretcher, and lift them into the ambulance. They're not thinking about whose fault it is. They aren't there to cast blame. They're there to help those who are hurting.

Now, there are also two types of ministries that I've observed. Those that take the attitude of the policeman. They come upon the tragedies, the broken lives, and they get out the code book. They're going to read you the law. *"You have the right to remain silent, but anything you say may be used against you."* They're on the scene in a very legal way trying to find out who's at fault, who's to blame, and to read the law.

But then there are those ministers who are more like the paramedics, and who aren't so concerned with who broke the law, but how they can heal. How can we help? How can we minister to the broken body, this broken life? How can we put things back together? How can we bring healing?

Now here in the account in John 8 are the Pharisees. They have the code book out. *"Our Law says stone her. What do you say?"* But Jesus was interested in ministering to her, helping her, putting her life back together, not condemning, *"Neither do I condemn thee."* His desire was to put her back on the road again.

We seek to minister to the hurting people. Our desire is to see them restored, back on their feet, functioning again. John tells us that the law came by Moses, but grace and truth came by Jesus Christ. If I am to be a minister of Jesus Christ, then I must be ministering grace. As we look at churches, and as we look at ministry, we see many who are principally ministers of Moses. They are very harsh and legalistic. The law has been broken, and they will tell you exactly what the law says. And, yet, we find Jesus saying,

"Whoever is without sin first cast the stone, ...neither do I condemn thee."

It's been our joy and our privilege to be able to restore many who were condemned by the law. I do believe that before restoration, there must be true repentance. I believe that the law was intended as a schoolmaster to bring people to Jesus Christ. Those who have not come and repented need the law, thus there is a place for the law. It is holy, righteous, and good, if used lawfully. But I think sometimes we go beyond and want to exact the penalties of the law after there has been repentance. We aren't willing to restore. Jesus stood for grace and truth. We should always seek restoration, but let us not forget that repentance is necessary.

It's wonderful to see a life that's been battered and bruised become fruitful again for the kingdom of God. But grace is not without risk. I may make a mistake in forgiving and showing grace to some people. It may be that their repentance isn't genuine. It may be that they still have a hidden agenda. I have shown grace to people who did prove to still be involved in sin, and who, later on, did damage to me. I'm not perfect. I've made mistakes in judgment and I've shown grace to those who had not truly repented of their evil.

I have taken chances, brought fellows on staff who had supposedly repented and later on, the same traits were still there. I've erred. And I probably will make mistakes in the future. But I will tell you this, if I'm going to err, I want to err on the side of grace rather than on the side of judgment.

In Ezekiel 34, the Lord spoke against the shepherds in Ezekiel. They had let the sheep go astray and didn't go out to seek the lost ones. The Lord had some pretty heavy things to say against those shepherds who weren't really concerned in seeking and restoring the lost ones. I believe God will be far more lenient with me and my errors of grace than He will be if it is the other way around and I condemn someone that He has pardoned and forgiven.

There are a several Scriptures that warn us against judgment. "Judge not, that ye be not judged." (Matt 7:1). We set the standard for our own judgment when we judge others. "Who art thou that judgest another man's servant? To his own master he standeth or falleth. Yea, he shall be holden up: for God is able to make him stand." (Romans 14:4). I would hate to err on the side of judgment, to judge someone falsely who had truly repented. I would hate to be in that position of making a mistake in my judgment. So again, if I err, I want to err on the side of grace because I know that God will be much more gracious towards me than if I err in judging a person wrongly. I don't want to be guilty of that.

It's easy to fall into legalism. We need to beware of this temptation. Beware of taking the hard stand. I have found, for the most part, that when a person gets heavy into 'Reformation Theology,' they usually get heavy into legalism. They want to make sure the 'T's' are crossed and the 'I's' are dotted just right. 'Reformation Theology' has some good points, but so does a porcupine. When you embrace it too forcefully, then you're going to get the points.

Some people object because they feel that I gloss over certain passages of Scripture, and they're correct. But glossing over controversial issues is often deliberate because there are usually two sides. And I have found that it's important not to be divisive and not to allow people to become polarized on issues, because the moment they are polarized, there's division.

A classic example is the problem in our understanding of the Scriptures that refer to the sovereignty of God and the responsibility of man. The Bible actually teaches both, but in our human understanding they're mutually exclusive. People who become divisive on this issue claim that we can't believe both, because if you carry the sovereignty of God to an extreme, it eliminates the responsibility of man. Likewise, if you carry the responsibilities of man to the extreme, it eliminates the sovereignty of God. This mistake is made when a person takes the doctrine and carries it out to its logical conclusion. Using human logic and carrying divine sovereignty out to its logical conclusion leaves man with no choices.

So, how are we to deal with rightly dividing the Word on the sovereignty of God and the responsibility of man? We need to believe both of them through faith, because I can't keep them in balance by my understanding. I don't understand how they come together. But I do believe them both. I believe that God is sovereign, and I also believe that I'm responsible and that God holds me responsible for the choices that I make. I simply trust God that both assertions of Scripture are true.

There's a pastor who recently came out with a little pamphlet on Calvinism, and on the front cover, there's a balance scale with John Calvin on one side and John 3:16 on the other. Which side would you rather stand for?

Don't get polarized. Don't let the people get polarized. The minute you do, you've lost half your congregation because people are split pretty evenly on this issue. So if you take a polarized position you'll lose half of your congregation. Do you really want to lose 50% of your congregation?

You know the beautiful thing about being called Calvary Chapel? People don't know where you really stand. Put Baptist in your title, and people know where you are, and half the people will never come because it's a Baptist church. Put Presbyterian in your name, and they know where you stand, and half the people will never come because they know what the Presbyterians believe. Put Nazarene in your name, and immediately they've got you pigeon-holed. They know who you are, and they don't need to go.

But Calvary Chapel has a sort of mystique about it. *"What do these people believe?" "I don't know, but let's go find out."* And the whole field is ours. You want to fish in as big a pond as you can find. When you're marketing something, you want the largest market appeal possible. So don't chop up the market and say, *"Well, we're just going to fish in this little market here."* Keep the market broad. Fish in the big pond. Fish where they are biting.

CHAPTER SIX

THE PRIORITY OF THE WORD

"Till I come, give attendance to reading, to exhortation, to doctrine."
1 Tim. 4:13

Another primary distinctive of Calvary Chapel is our endeavor to declare to people the whole counsel of God. We see this principle illustrated when Paul met with the Ephesian elders in Acts 20. As they were on the shore of the Aegean at Miletus, around the coastal area of Ephesus, Paul said that he was innocent of the blood of all men, *"For I have not shunned to declare unto you all the counsel of God."* (Acts 20:27).

Now, how is it possible for a person to claim to have declared, *"the whole counsel of God?"* The only way a person could make that claim to his congregation would be if he taught through the whole Word of God with them, from Genesis to Revelation. Once you've taken your congregation through the Bible, then you can say to them, *" I have not shunned to declare unto you the whole counsel of God."*

This can't be done with topical sermons. Topical sermons are good, and they have their place, but when you're preaching topically, you're prone by nature to preach only those topics that you like. And there are topics in the Bible that aren't very inspiring. They don't excite the people, but they are necessary issues that have to be dealt with. The human tendency, however, is to avoid these. If you're only preaching topically, you may also tend to avoid controversial or difficult topics, and the people won't gain a well-balanced view of God's truth. So the value of going straight through the Bible is that you can say, *"I have not shunned to declare to you all the counsel of God."*

Now, I believe that I can say to the people at Calvary Chapel Costa Mesa, *"I have declared unto you the whole counsel of God,"* because we have taken them from Genesis to Revelation seven times. We're currently beginning the eighth round. We don't skip anything. And that's why in the majority of the Calvary Chapels, and the most successful ones, you'll find the systematic teaching of the entire Word of God, going through the Bible from cover to cover.

For the most part, the teaching ministry of Calvary Chapel is expositional in style. It doesn't mean that on occasion we don't address a particular topic or give topical messages. We're not saying that topical messages are wrong or evil. They have their place. We don't want to fall into strict legalism where we analyze every sermon to see if it was homiletically correct and expositionally presented. But, for the most part, we seek to follow the example of Isaiah who said, "But the word of the LORD was unto them precept upon precept, precept upon precept; line upon line, line upon line; here a little, and there a little;" (Isaiah 28:13). These verses are describing the people's reaction to Isaiah's style of teaching.

They were making fun of his method, but it was an effective method. They were complaining about him, mockingly saying that he ought go back and teach the kindergartners because his teaching was "precept upon precept; line upon line, line upon line; here a little, and there a little." They said these words in derision. Yet, it's so important to take the people through the Word, line upon line, precept by precept. When we do, we are delivering to them the whole counsel of God.

Another advantage of teaching the whole counsel of God is that when you come to difficult issues that deal with problems in an individual's life or within the Church body, you can address them straightforwardly. We need not worry about people thinking, *"Oh, he's aiming at me today."* People in the congregation know that it's simply the passage of Scripture being studied that day. So it can't be, *"Oh man, he's really picking on me,"* because they realize that you're going straight through the Book, and you're not jumping from topic to topic. We're just going straight through the entire Word of God.

In Nehemiah chapter 8 verse 8, when the children of Israel had returned from captivity and were rebuilding the city, the leadership gathered the people together and constructed a little platform. They began in the early morning to read the Word of God to the people. Nemehiah 8:8 declares, "So they read in the book in the law of God distinctly, and gave the sense, and caused them to understand the reading."

I believe this is a worthy definition of expositional preaching—to read the Word, give the sense, and cause the people to understand the meaning. I have found that many times I really don't begin to grasp the meaning until I have read a particular passage maybe 50 or 60 times. Suddenly it begins to come together in my own mind. I believe it's valuable to use good commentaries to help in understanding the meaning of a passage. I appreciate the insights God has given to other men on passages of the Word. But in saying that I appreciate and do read commentaries, I must also confess that often I will read pages and pages from commentaries and get absolutely nothing that I can use. Sometimes when you read seven commentaries on a particular passage, you're more confused when you're through than when you started, because there are so many different concepts or ideas on a particular passage. So I believe that one of the best commentaries on the Bible is the Bible itself.

It is important to remember that we don't generally see immediate or spectacular overnight results in a Calvary Chapel. It takes time to whet and develop the appetite of the people for the Word of God. It takes time for them to grow. For most Calvary Chapels that are planted in a new area, it takes a couple of years to lay the foundation, prepare the ground, plow the hardened soil, work the soil, and plant the seed in the fertile soil. Then you have to wait. The seed doesn't bear fruit overnight. The seed has to grow and to develop. But, eventually, it begins to bear fruit.

Most of the fellows that I have observed have gone out and by the end of the second year, they've hit the crisis point. They're usually discouraged. They feel it isn't going to happen where they are. They start believing that the people there are different from other people, and that it's just not going to happen. You'd be amazed at how many have gone out, and after two years have called me up saying they were going to be leaving because it just wasn't happening. I'll encourage them to stay for just another six months or so, telling them, "Look, you've come through the hard part. You've been through the plowing. You've been through the cultivating of the soil. You've been through the planting. Now wait and watch and see if any fruit will come forth." As a general rule, it's in the third year that you begin to see fruit as a result of planting the

Word of God in the hearts of the people. "The seed that falls on good soil will bring forth fruit, some thirty, some sixty, some a hundred fold," (Matthew 13:8). But it doesn't happen overnight.

This can be rather discouraging when there are those who come in with a flash and a fire, and seem to generate an immediate crowd. People are thronging to see the miracles, to watch the fireworks, and here you are just plodding along. You can't see much development or growth, and these other guys seem to have instant success. But as the Lord said to Daniel, "And they that be wise shall shine as the brightness of the firmament; and they that turn many to righteousness as the stars for ever and ever." (Daniel 12:3).

On the Fourth of July it's fun to watch the fireworks, the sky rockets, the blazes of glory, and all the color filling the sky. Everybody is *"oohing and aahing,"* but it only lasts for a short time. Before you know it, it's just ashes. It's a big flash, and then it's all over. That's the way many ministries are, just a big flash and then it's over. You have to determine which sky you want to shine in. Do you want to shine as a star for ever and ever? Or do you want to be like a sky rocket with a sudden flash, coming on the scene dramatically, but with no staying power?

CHAPTER SEVEN

THE CENTRALITY OF JESUS CHRIST

"For we preach not ourselves, but Christ Jesus the Lord..."
2 Cor. 4:5

One of the important characteristics of Calvary Chapel is the centrality of Jesus Christ in our worship. We don't allow any practice or behavior that would distract people from focusing on Him. For example, we don't allow people to stand up individually when we're singing in the church. The moment a person stands, those near him become aware of him and begin to wonder, *"Why is he standing?"* The focus is taken off Jesus and placed onto the person who's standing.

The eye is interesting because it's attracted to motion. In many cases, I've seen those, who stand up by themselves in worship, conclude they're not getting quite enough attention so they raise their hands and start to sway. That's eye-catching. But it's also a distraction, and suddenly people are wondering why they're standing there. *"What are they thinking? Are they aware that they're drawing attention to themselves? What's going on?"* I believe that it's important for these things to be dealt with because displays like these will cause you to lose prospective members to the church. If I went into a church and that was happening, I might think that the sermon was great, but I can't quite handle all these other things.

I was in a Calvary Chapel a while back and they did allow the people to stand individually. Unfortunately, what one does, others usually do. They had one fellow every night who was down in the front row, and he was more than just standing. He was really dancing down there. It was obvious that the fellow didn't have all of his marbles, and he no doubt had certain psychological needs. He found an environment where he could do his little weird things and be accepted, but it was extremely distracting. I spoke to the pastor about it, and he defended the practice, so I thought, "All right, stay small".

At Calvary Chapel Costa Mesa, if someone does stand up, the ushers approach them and invite them back to the foyer, then one of the pastors talks to them there, gently and in love. They usually say, "We don't practice this because we've discovered that it draws people's attention away from worship. And surely you wouldn't want to take the person's attention from Jesus Christ and put it on yourself, would you?"

We tell them they are drawing attention to themselves, and people are losing the central focus on Jesus. We talk to them in love and suggest that they not do it, and if they get upset it shows that they were in the flesh the whole time. If they're really in the Spirit and walking in the Spirit, they will take it in the Spirit. They'll say, "Oh, I didn't realize that. I'm sorry." But if they get all huffy, then you know that they were in the flesh.

Jesus said, "Take heed that ye do not your alms before men, to be seen of them: otherwise ye have no reward of your Father which is in heaven." (Matthew 6:1). He then illustrated how people sought to bring attention to themself as they performed their righteous acts of worship. Like it or not, if you're standing and swaying when everyone else is sitting it will attract attention to you.

I was in another Calvary Chapel where they had these ladies dressed in granny outfits with bonnets doing interpretive dancing to the worship choruses down at the front. Now, if ever there was anything that was distracting to me, that was it. They were pretty good as far as graceful movements, but I found that I really didn't get much out of the worship choruses that night. I watched these ladies and their graceful movements, just trying to understand their interpretation of the songs. So, again I spoke to the pastor afterwards, and he got the picture and has since stopped this interpretive dancing, realizing that it was distracting.

We had an affiliate church in Basil, Switzerland that was probably one of the most exciting churches in Europe. As far as potential, and as far as what was happening, I believe it was perhaps the largest Protestant church in Europe at the time. Every year I would go over to Basil and speak in their fellowship. It was really exciting. They had caught the whole Calvary Chapel vision. They had choruses, a great worship group, and the teaching of the Word. They had hundreds and hundreds of young people who were coming on Sunday nights to the beautiful gothic style church. The state church had allowed them to use the facility. The state church was using it only on Sunday mornings. Since only six elderly people attended, the Bishop said that our Calvary Chapel could use it on Sunday nights. It was jammed to the rafters and really had a great outreach doing a vital work. They had opened up a coffee shop. They had a great program going. They were dealing with the hippie, drug-oriented kids. The church was located in the center of a drug-infested area, and the kids that were being saved needed housing, so the church provided it for them. The church had also developed factories to manufacture various types of novelty souvenirs, and that was a successful venture, too. The kids were employed and those with artistic gifts were able to use their painting ability. It was going great guns.

The last time I was there they had gotten into interpretive dancing with a couple of gals in leotards. They had brought in an assistant pastor from a Pentecostal background, and they had gotten into this business of standing. The pastor was not strong enough to deal with it. I talked to him after the service and I said, "This stuff has to go. It's going to destroy you." Actually, he wasn't even in control of the meeting. I noticed that when the time had come for me to be introduced to speak, these gals went up, whispered in his ear, and then they sang one more chorus and performed one more dance. The dancers were in control of the meeting, not the pastor. So I talked to him about it, but he was reluctant to really face up to the issue. As a result, we don't have any church in Basil today. He left, the Pentecostals took over, the church kicked them out, and now there is no work going on there.

So it's important that we keep Jesus Christ as the central focus and keep distractions to a minimum. When distractions do take place, deal with them and if necessary publicly talk about them.

When I was in Bible College, there was a fellow who would always sit down in the front row. Usually at one of the most powerful moments in the service, when the Spirit of God was really working in the people's hearts, he would lean down towards the floor, and then he would stand up, hands raised, yelling, *"Hallelujah!"* Everybody would laugh. But then everybody's attention was on this character crying, *"Hallelujah!"* The point of the sermon was lost. He destroyed so many sermons because of his actions. So I determined I was going to stop it! I sat in the row right behind him, and when he leaned over to go into his *"Hallelujah"* bit, I grabbed his shoulders and began to pinch a nerve, and held him down on his knees. Nobody else had the courage to stop him. They just let it go on and on, and it was such a distracting thing!

A few years back I was in Colorado Springs at a retreat, and there was a man down in the front who was sort of a simpleton. You could tell just by looking at him. While we're all singing worship choruses, this man was dancing up and down in the aisle. I asked the pastor, "Why do you allow that?" He said, "Well, they wanted to have freedom..." I replied, "Look, that isn't freedom. If I were a stranger coming to your church for the first time, and saw this guy down there, I wouldn't come back. I'd think your fellowship was weird!"

We get to the place where we accept things that are wrong because we don't have the courage to stop them. We're afraid of being accused of quenching the Spirit. I will quench that kind of spirit! Not the Holy Spirit, but the spirit that is seeking to bring attention to an individual, distracting people from the worship of the Lord.

In the past (and this has not happened at Calvary for a long time) we've had people get up during the service and try to give an utterance in tongues. Again, the ushers were right on top of it. They invited them back to the foyer, and the pastors explained to them that at Calvary we don't allow public utterances in tongues or public prophecies, as in the Charismatic or Pentecostal churches. From the pulpit I then explained to the congregation that the gift of tongues is valid in the New Testament, and that there is a proper place for tongues. I explained that Paul pointed out that, in his personal experience, he would rather speak five words in a known tongue than ten thousand in an unknown tongue when he's in the church. Yet, he was thankful that he spoke in tongues more than all of them. In your private devotions, it's a very edifying experience. It's a means by which you can praise God and worship God. But with a church the size of Calvary Chapel, and some people not being able to hear the interpretation at all, it's not edifying in our public services to exercise this particular gift of the Spirit, even with an interpretation. It isn't edifying or convenient, so we don't do it. We don't allow it during the public services, but we encourage the person to use and exercise the gift in their own personal devotional life.

If you have a group of believers and you're gathered for prayer to seek the Lord, then the use of the gift of tongues is allowable with interpretation. But I believe, that when there are unbelievers present, it creates confusion and questions. Therefore, it's best to confine it to believers who are gathered together specifically to wait on the Lord, like we do in an afterglow setting. It's edifying and allowable there. People are simply seeking the Lord and the fullness of His Spirit, so in that environment it's allowable.

Paul said in 1 Corinthians 1:29, *"No flesh should glory in His presence."* I wonder if we realize just how serious a thing it is to try and bring attention to ourselves in the presence of the Lord? Do we really want to distract peoples attention away from Jesus Christ and draw it to ourselves? I think that's a very serious offense. And I surely wouldn't want to be guilty of it.

In the Old Testament we find a very interesting case of just how serious this is. When Israel had completed the Tabernacle and all of the furnishings for it, they gathered the people together to dedicate and to begin offering sacrifices. The congregation of Israel was assembled and everybody was in place. Aaron was in his priestly robes, as were his sons, and the whole scene, according to the plan of God, was all in order. Then, suddenly, as the people were there waiting to start things, the fire of God came and kindled the fire on the altar. It was spontaneous combustion. All of the people saw this sign of God's presence and broke forth with great shouting. There was great excitement everywhere, and boundless emotion at the realization that God was present among His people. Then the two sons of Aaron, Nadab and Abihu, took false fire and put it in their incense burners. They started to go in to offer this incense before the Lord inside the Holy place. Then Scripture says that fire came from the altar and consumed Nadab and Abihu. (Leviticus 10).

It's my belief that they got caught up in the emotion and the excitement of the moment. They were going to demonstrate to the people their position as priests and how important "_we_ are." As a result, they were consumed.

I'm very leery of strange fire. You also want to be very careful about strange fire—those emotions that don't stem from God Himself, and the kind of service that doesn't originate with God. It's an endeavor to draw attention to the instrument rather than to the Master.

We see this in the early church with Ananias and Sapphira. Here again is an attempt to draw praise and glory to the individual. Ananias and Sapphira had sold their property and brought a portion of the proceeds they received to the church, but they pretended they were giving everything. I believe this was to draw the praise and the awe of the people, who would then say, "Look at that, they're giving everything to God!", when in reality they were holding back.

We all like that kind of attention. We like it when people think we're spiritual. Be careful! Our flesh is so rotten. I want to be known as a deeply spiritual person. My flesh revels in people thinking that I'm really more spiritual than I am. Sometimes we purposefully try to give off this impression, and I think this has been one of the curses of the church. Some pastors seek to present an image of deep spirituality that just isn't real.

It begins to affect their actions. They begin to get a voice that sounds so holy, they hold their hands in a special way, and then they say, *"Oh, dear sister, tell me all about it."* Their whole manner changes and their demeanor gives off an impression of a holy man. And they love it. They love people to think they're spiritual giants. They want people to want to know the Word like they know it, or to think that they spend hours in prayer. They just smile and say, *"It takes a lot of commitment, you know."*

We really need to be cautious about creating an aura around ourselves and loving the adulation that comes from people. In the case of Ananias and Sapphira, they were zapped because they drew the attention and glory to themselves, the glory that should have been going to the Lord. And they paid a severe price. God doesn't want to share His glory. Be careful! Don't allow things that can distract. We want to keep Jesus as the central focus for the people. It's very important to keep Jesus Christ as the central focus in our worship.

CHAPTER EIGHT

THE RAPTURE OF THE CHURCH

"Looking for that blessed hope, and the glorious appearing of the great God and our Saviour Jesus Christ."
Titus 2:13

The Rapture refers to that time when Jesus is going to come, without warning, and take away His church from this earth. After the Rapture, the Lord will pour out His wrath upon this sinful world. There are many pastors who claim an ignorance of the Rapture or say that they are not certain whether it will precede the Tribulation. They say they don't really know where they stand on this issue. I don't believe there is any excuse for not having a position on this issue. We have our Bibles and we're capable of studying this subject thoroughly. I believe that your view of the Rapture will have a significant impact on the success of your ministry.

First of all, we know that Jesus promised He would come again. In John 14 we read, "Let not your heart be troubled: ye believe in God, believe also in me. In my Father's house are many mansions: if it were not so, I would have told you. I go to prepare a place for you. And if I go and prepare a place for you, I will come again, and receive you unto myself; that where I am, there ye may be also." (John 14:1-3). The Lord promises to come again and to receive His disciples unto Himself, that where He is we might be also.

Paul, in writing to the Corinthians declared, "Behold, I show you a mystery." (1 Corinthians15:51). A mystery in the New Testament means something that has not yet been revealed by God in His progressive revelation of Himself, His purposes, and plans to man.

Paul, for instance, spoke to the Colossians about, "What is the riches of the glory of this mystery among the Gentiles; which is Christ in you, the hope of glory." (Colossians 1:27). The Old Testament prophets did not comprehend what it meant that Christ would be in us. Even the angels desire to fully grasp these things. (1 Peter 1:12). In the 1 Corinthians 15:51 passage we are introduced to another never before revealed truth, "Behold, I show you a mystery; We shall not all sleep, but we shall all be changed, In a moment, in the twinkling of an eye, at the last trump."

When the Bible declares that we will "all be changed," it means there will be a metamorphosis. "For this corruptible must put on incorruption, and this mortal must put on immortality." (1Corinthians 15:53). All believers will go through a glorious change at the coming of Jesus Christ for His church.

The Thessalonians were having a problem with this issue. Paul only ministered there for a couple of weeks, but in that short time he taught them many things. One of the things he taught them concerned the Rapture of the church. The Thessalonians were looking for the coming Kingdom.

I believe it is God's intention that every church age be convinced they are the last generation. I also believe that God's divine design is for the church to live in constant expectancy of the Lord's return. Jesus, talking about His return, said, "Blessed is that servant, whom his lord when he cometh shall find so doing." (Matthew 24:46).

The early church believed that Jesus would set up the Kingdom immediately. In the first chapter of Acts, the disciples asked, "Lord, wilt thou at this time restore again the kingdom to Israel?" (Acts 1:6). "Are we just a few days away?" They were excited because they were expecting the Lord to set up the Kingdom at any time.

Jesus responded by saying, "It is not for you to know the times or the seasons, which the Father hath put in his own power. But ye shall receive power, after that the Holy Ghost is come upon you." (Acts 1:7-8).

There was a rumor in the early church that the Lord would come back before John died. Every time John got a cold or sore throat the whole church would get excited. So John wrote in the Gospel to clarify what Jesus had said. Jesus was telling Peter how He would die, and then Peter, in his typical manner, said, "But, Lord, what about him?" Jesus responded, "If I will that he tarry till I come, what is that to thee? Follow thou Me." (John 21:22). John took note of the point that Jesus didn't say that He was going to, He said, "If I will." So John sought to correct the mistaken notion that Jesus would come before he died.

The Thessalonians were looking for the Lord to come, but some of their dear brethren in the church at Thessalonica had died, and still Jesus had not returned. They believed that because they had died before Jesus came back, they would miss out on the glorious Kingdom. In 1 Thessalonians chapter 4, Paul corrected this mistaken idea that if a person died before Jesus came back, they would miss out on the Kingdom. So he said, "I would not have you to be ignorant, brethren, concerning them which are asleep, that ye sorrow not, even as others which have no hope." (1 Thessalonians 4:13). Paul went on to say, "For if we believe that Jesus died and rose again, even so them also which sleep in Jesus will God bring with him. For this we say unto you by the word of the Lord, that we which are alive and remain unto the coming of the Lord shall not prevent them which are asleep." (1 Thessalonians 4:14-15) Paul believed that he would probably be alive and remain until the coming of the Lord. He emphasized that we would not precede those who sleep. "For the Lord himself shall descend from heaven with a shout, with the voice of the archangel, and with the trump of God: and the dead in Christ shall rise first: Then we which are alive and remain shall be caught up together with them in the clouds, to meet the Lord in the air: and so shall we ever be with the Lord. Wherefore comfort one another with these words." (1 Thessalonians 4:16-18).

There are people who say, "I don't believe in the Rapture of the church," because they have looked through the Bible and have never found the word "Rapture" in the Bible. But in I Thessalonians 4:17 we read that, "Then we which are alive and remain shall be *caught up* together with them in the clouds, to meet the Lord in the air: and so shall we ever be with the Lord."

The word translated 'caught up' in the Greek is 'harpazo,' which means 'to be taken away by force.' It's usually used as a military term related to the taking of hostages. The Latin Vulgate translates 'harpazo' as 'raptuse,' and that's where we get our English word 'rapture.' Jesus will return to rapture His church. That's the first event.

The second event is the Second Coming of Jesus Christ, when He comes again with His church to establish His Kingdom upon the earth. The Rapture then is distinct from the Second Coming of Jesus Christ. We're told, "Behold, he cometh with clouds; and every eye shall see him, and they also which pierced him: and all kindreds of the earth shall wail because of him. Even so, Amen." (Revelation 1:7). And, "When Christ, who is our life, shall appear, then shall ye also appear with him in glory." (Colossians 3:4). The Second Coming of Jesus will be to establish God's Kingdom upon the earth. But prior to that Second Coming there will be an event when the church will be caught up to be with the Lord. The thing I love most about this event is that, "so shall we ever be with the Lord." (1 Thessalonians 4:17).

There is a distinct difference between Jesus coming **for** His church and Jesus coming **with** His church. He will be coming for His church at the Rapture. But at the Second Coming of Jesus, He'll be coming with His church. "When Christ, who is our life, shall appear," (at His Second Coming) "then shall ye also appear with him in glory." (Colossians 3:4).

Jude 14 speaks of the Second Coming when it states, "Enoch also, the seventh from Adam, prophesied of these, saying, Behold, the Lord cometh with ten thousands of his saints." Zechariah also spoke of this when he wrote, "And his feet shall stand in that day upon the Mount of Olives, which is before Jerusalem on the east, and the mount of Olives shall cleave in the midst thereof toward the east and toward the west, and there shall be a very great valley; and half of the mountain shall remove toward the north, and half of it toward the south. And ye shall flee to the valley of the mountains; for the valley of the mountains shall reach unto Azal: yea, ye shall flee, like as ye fled from before the earthquake in the days of

Uzziah king of Judah: and the LORD my God shall come, and all the saints with thee." (Zechariah 14:4-5).

The Rapture can take place at any time. There are no prophecies that have yet to be fulfilled before the Rapture occurs. It could happen before you're through reading this chapter, and we would be thrilled if it did!

There are some prophecies that are yet to be fulfilled before Jesus comes again. The Antichrist must be revealed, and the earth must go through a time of great tribulation and judgment. These prophecies relate specifically to the Second Coming of Jesus. Jesus spoke about the signs of His coming in Luke 21:28, "And when these things begin to come to pass, (the signs of His Second Coming) then look up, and lift up your heads; for your redemption draweth nigh."

Last year, towards the end of October, just before Halloween, I was going by a major mall in Southern California and saw them putting up the Santa Claus, the reindeer, and other Christmas decorations, but it was still October. I said to my wife, "Look at that! They're putting up Christmas decorations! That's great! I love Thanksgiving!" She responded, "Those aren't Thanksgiving decorations! They're Christmas decorations!" I said, "I know that! But, I also know that Thanksgiving comes before Christmas. So if the signs of Christmas are up, Thanksgiving's getting close!" And, in the same way, when we see the signs of the Second Coming, we know that the Rapture's getting close.

Jesus had given His disciples the signs of His coming in response to their question, "Tell us, when shall these things be? And what shall be the sign of thy coming, and of the end of the world?" (Matthew 24:3). Jesus had just walked through the temple with His disciples and they were remarking on how huge the stones were. Jesus said, "There shall not be left here one stone upon another, that shall not be thrown down." (Matthew 24:2). When they got over to the Mount of Olives, they asked Jesus, "What shall be the sign of thy coming, and of the end of the world?" (Matthew 24:3). So they weren't asking for just one set of signs. They were asking for signs of the destruction of the temple, and they were also asking about the signs of the end of this current age of human government and the coming of the Kingdom of God.

They didn't ask about, nor did they probably even understand, the Rapture of the church. But Jesus proceeded to give them the signs of the destruction of the temple and the signs of His coming again. When He speaks about the signs of His Second Coming, He naturally speaks about the Great Tribulation. "For then shall be great tribulation, such as was not since the beginning of the world to this time, no, nor ever shall be." (Matthew 24:21). Jesus also warns them, "When ye therefore shall see the abomination of desolation, spoken of by Daniel the prophet, stand in the holy place, (whoso readeth, let him understand:)" (Matthew 24:15). When you see that abomination standing in the holy place, you'll know it's time for you to get out of Jerusalem and flee to the wilderness. And then, "Immediately after the tribulation of those days shall the sun be darkened, and the moon shall not give her light, and the stars shall fall from heaven, and the powers of the heavens shall be shaken: And then shall appear the sign of the Son of man in heaven: and then shall all the tribes of the earth mourn, and they shall see the Son of man coming in the clouds of heaven with power and great glory." (Matthew 24:29-30).

Prior to the Second Coming, there are many prophecies that must be fulfilled. There must be the revelation of the Antichrist and the establishing of Satan's kingdom in full power during the Great Tribulation. These events must occur before the Second Coming of Jesus. But there is nothing that must occur before the Rapture of the church. That is why we are told to watch and be ready, "for in such an hour as ye think not the Son of man cometh." Therefore, "Blessed is that servant, whom his lord when he cometh shall find so doing." (Matthew 24:44,46).

Jesus then began to tell them a series of parables. The point of each parable in the series is to watch and be ready for His return at any time. Each parable focuses on the key point that the Rapture is imminent, that is, it can happen at any time.

In the Parable of the Ten Virgins we read, "And five of them were wise, and five were foolish." (Matthew 25:2). Those "that were ready went in with him to the marriage: and the door was shut. Afterward came also the other virgins, saying, Lord, Lord, open to us. But he answered and said, Verily I say unto you, I know you not. Watch therefore, for ye know neither the day nor the hour wherein the Son of man cometh." (Matthew 25:10-13). The emphasis throughout is to watch and be ready, because you don't know when the Lord is coming for His servants.

In Matthew 24:42-44 we read, "Watch therefore: for ye know not what hour your Lord doth come. But know this, that if the goodman of the house had known in what watch the thief would come, he would have watched, and would not have suffered his house to be broken up. Therefore be ye also ready: for in such an hour as ye think not the Son of man cometh."

I firmly believe that the church will not go through the Great Tribulation. Talking about the Tribulation in Luke 21, Jesus said, "Watch ye therefore, and pray always, that ye may be accounted worthy to escape all these things that shall come to pass, and to stand before the Son of man." (Luke 21:36). Now if Jesus tells me to pray for something, believe me, I will do it! I pray, "Lord, I want to be accounted worthy to escape these things that will come to pass upon the earth." This is in the context of the Great Tribulation.

We're told in Revelation 1:19 that the book is divided into three sections. "Write the things which thou hast seen, and the things which are, and the things which shall be hereafter." In chapter one, John was told to, "Write the things which thou hast seen", and he wrote about the vision he saw of Christ walking in the midst of the seven golden candlesticks, holding the seven stars in His right hand. He wrote about the glorious description of Jesus in His glorified state.

In chapters two and three, he writes about the "things that are." This refers to messages of Jesus to the seven churches of Asia. I believe that these were seven actual churches of that day, but I also believe that they refer to seven periods of church history. I also believe they are representative of churches that you can find today.

There are churches today that have left their first love. There are churches today that have embraced the doctrine of the Nicolaitans. There's a suffering church of Smryna in the world today such as those suffering persecution in China, Sudan, and other places. I believe that there's the church of Thyratira that has embodied the doctrine of "Mariology." We can see the church of Sardis portrayed in dead Protestantism, "thou hast a name that thou livest, and art dead." (Revelation 3:1).

I believe that there is the Philadelphian church, that church which is staying true to the Word. It may not have much power, but thank God that He has "set before thee an open door, and no man can shut it: for thou hast a little strength, and hast kept my word, and hast not denied my name." (Revelation 3:8). We may not be big or earth shaking, but thank God we are making a little impression!

But there is also the Laodicean church, the one that has put Jesus outside. He's standing at the door and knocking, and saying, "If any man hear my voice, and open the door, I will come in to him, and will sup with him, and he with me." (Revelation 3:20).

So I believe that you have a three-fold application for the messages to the seven churches. In chapter four, verse one, when He's finished with the messages to the churches, He introduces a new section with the Greek word, 'metatauta' (after these things), that He also used in 1:19. We need to ask, "After what things?" After the things of chapters two and three. The things of chapters two and three are the things of the church. So after the things that pertain to the church we read, "After this I looked, and, behold, a door was opened in heaven: and the first voice which I heard was as it were of a trumpet talking with me; which said, Come up hither, and I will shew thee things which must be hereafter." (Revelation 4:1).

After this command, John said, "Immediately I was in the spirit: and, behold, a throne was set in heaven, and One sat on the throne." (Revelation 4:2). He then describes the throne of God with its emerald rainbow round about and the cherubim as they are worshiping. He sees the twenty four lesser thrones with the elders sitting on them and watches and observes the heavenly worship as the cherubim are declaring the eternal character, nature, and holiness of God. "They rest not day and night, saying, Holy, holy, holy, Lord God Almighty, which was, and is, and is to come." (Revelation 4:8). As they are declaring the holiness of God, the twenty four elders fall on their faces, take their golden crowns, cast them on the glassy sea, and declare, "Thou art worthy, O Lord, to receive glory and honour and power: for thou hast created all things, and for thy pleasure they are and were created." (Revelation 4:11).

Then John's attention is drawn to a sealed scroll with seven seals, with writing on the inside and the outside. An angel proclaims with a loud voice, "Who is worthy to open the book, and to loose the seals thereof?" (Revelation 5:2). And John writes, "And I wept much, because no man was found worthy to open and to read the book, neither to look thereon." (Revelation 5:4). It is my belief that this scroll is the title deed to the earth, according to the Jewish Law of Redemption. There was an established time when you could redeem forfeited or lost property provided you fulfilled the requirements within the deed, represented by the scroll. We see this illustrated in the story of Ruth when Boaz redeemed the field that belonged to Elimelech in order that he might obtain the bride. We also see this illustrated in Jesus who purchased and paid the price to redeem the world in order that He might have His bride, the church.

Back in heaven, we find John weeping because, under Jewish law, if you don't redeem property at that appointed time, it goes to the new owner perpetually. You have one opportunity, after that it permanently belongs to the new owner. The thought of the world being forever under Satan's power and control was more than John could handle, and he begins to sob convulsively, until an elder says, "Weep not: behold, the Lion of the tribe of Juda, the Root of David, hath prevailed to open the book, and to loose the seven seals thereof." (Revelation 5:5). John says that he didn't see Him as a Lion of the tribe of Judah. He saw Him as a Lamb that had been slaughtered. Isaiah says, "For he shall grow up before him as a tender plant, and as a root out of a dry ground: he hath no form nor comeliness; and when we shall see him, there is no beauty that we should desire him... But he was wounded for our transgressions, he was bruised for our iniquities: the chastisement of our peace was upon him; and with his stripes we are healed." (Isaiah 53:2,5).

In Revelation chapter five we read, "And he came and took the book out of the right hand of him that sat upon the throne. And when he had taken the book, the four beasts and four and twenty elders fell down before the Lamb, having every one of them harps, and golden vials full of odours, which are the prayers of saints. And they sang a new song, saying, Thou art worthy to take the book, and to open the seals thereof: for thou wast slain, and hast redeemed us to God by thy blood out of every kindred, and tongue, and people, and nation; And hast made us unto our God kings and priests: and we shall reign on the earth." (Revelation 5:7-10).

As you look carefully at the lyrics, we realize that only the church can sing them. When the Lord is in heaven receiving the title deed to the earth, we will be in heaven watching Him as He takes the scroll out of the right hand of Him who is sitting on the throne. We will join in a glorious chorus singing, "Thou art worthy to take the book, and to open the seals thereof: for thou wast slain, and hast redeemed us to God by thy blood out of every kindred, and tongue, and people, and nation." (Revelation 5:9). In Luke 21, Jesus told His disciples about the signs of His Second Coming and the Great Tribulation that would precede the end of the age. He said, "Watch ye therefore, and pray always, that ye may be accounted worthy to escape all these things that shall come to pass, and to stand before the Son of man." (Luke 21:36).

When the Great Tribulation occurs on earth, I expect to be in heaven standing before the Son of Man and singing of the worthiness of the Lamb. Only the church can sing this song of redemption. If we follow the timing, we see that the church singing the song of redemption occurs in chapter five, before the opening of the scroll in chapter six, and that precedes the Great Tribulation on the earth. Again we read that He has "redeemed us to God by thy blood out of every kindred, and tongue, and people, and nation; And hast made us unto our God kings and priests: and we shall reign on the earth." (Revelation 5:9-10).

We see the church standing before the Son of Man and Jesus, talking about the Great Tribulation, saying, "Pray always that you may be counted worthy to escape all these things that will come to pass, and to stand before the Son of Man." (Luke 21:36). Believe me, I want to be in that company up there!

Revelation chapter six begins the description of the Great Tribulation. As the Lord opens each seal of the scroll, a corresponding judgment is released upon the earth. As the first seal is opened, John writes, "And I saw, and behold a white horse: and he that sat on him had a bow; and a crown was given unto him: and he went forth conquering, and to conquer." (Revelation 6:2). I believe this is the revelation of the Antichrist. Some believe this rider on the white horse is Jesus Christ! But, as we examine the passage, we see that it's followed by war, famine, bloodshed, and a fourth of the people being killed. That doesn't sound like the Kingdom of God and the glorious coming of the Lord! I believe it is the Antichrist.

I do believe that the forces and the power of the Antichrist are in the world today and that the only thing keeping them from taking over is the presence of the church. We have a little strength, not much, but enough to keep back the powers of darkness from taking complete control. I don't believe that the Antichrist can take over until the church is removed.

Paul tells us in 2 Thessalonians chapter 2, "For the mystery of iniquity doth already work: only he who now letteth will let, until he be taken out of the way. And then shall that Wicked be revealed, whom the

Lord shall consume with the spirit of his mouth, and shall destroy with the brightness of his coming:" (2 Thessalonians 2:7-8). This lines up with the Revelation chapter six passage where the church is in heaven as Jesus takes the scroll. As He begins to loose the scroll, the corresponding judgments are released upon the earth. It is the time of the pouring out of God's wrath.

In Romans 5:9, Paul tells us that, " Much more then, being now justified by his blood, we shall be saved from wrath through him." He repeats this in 1 Thessalonians 5:9, "For God hath not appointed us to wrath, but to obtain salvation by our Lord Jesus Christ."

We, the church, are not "appointed unto wrath." In Romans 1, Paul writes, "For the wrath of God is revealed from heaven against all ungodliness and unrighteousness of men, who hold the truth in unrighteousness;" (Romans 1:18). It simply isn't consistent with the nature of God to judge the righteous with the wicked.

Now it is true that in the world we Christians will have tribulation. The world hates us, so we shouldn't be surprised at persecution. Jesus said, "If the world hate you, ye know that it hated me before it hated you" (John 15:18), and "In the world ye shall have tribulation: but be of good cheer; I have overcome the world." (John 16:33). So, in this world you will have tribulation. But what is the source of the tribulation against the church? It's not God! Satan is the source of the tribulation.

When Satan is the source of tribulation, you can expect the children of God to be those who will be persecuted. But when God is the source of the judgment, it's a different story. God has already judged our sins on the cross of Jesus Christ. Jesus bore the judgment of God for all of our guilt.

Remember when the angels were on their way to destroy Sodom? They stopped by and visited Abraham. They said, "Should we tell Abraham what we're about to do?" And they decided, "Well, why not?" So they told him that the sin of Sodom had ascended up into heaven and that they were on their way to check out the reports and destroy the city.

Abraham asked them to wait because his nephew Lot was living there. He said, "Would You also destroy the righteous with the wicked? Suppose there were fifty righteous within the city; would You also destroy the place and not spare it for the fifty righteous that were in it?' So the LORD said, 'If I find in Sodom fifty righteous within the city, then I will spare all the place for their sake.' Then Abraham answered and said, 'Suppose there were five less than the fifty righteous; would You destroy all of the city for lack of five?' So He said, 'If I find there forty-five, I will not destroy it.' 'Suppose there should be forty found there?' So He said, 'I will not do it for the sake of forty.' 'Suppose thirty should be found there?' So He said, 'I will not do it if I find thirty there.' 'Suppose twenty should be found there?' So He said, 'I will not destroy it for the sake of twenty.' 'Suppose ten should be found there?' And He said, 'I will not destroy it for the sake of ten.' (Genesis 18:23-33).

And what happened? When the angels came to the city of Sodom, they found one righteous man, Lot, sitting at the gate. Lot knew what the Sodomites were like. We're told by Peter that his righteous spirit had been vexed by the way the people were living. Lot, not knowing these individuals were angels, invited them into his home. That night the men of Sodom came and began to beat on the door, saying, "Where are the men which came in to thee this night? bring them out unto us, that we may know them." (Genesis 19:5). They literally wanted to rape them. Lot replied, "I pray you, brethren, do not so wickedly." (Genesis 19:7).

The angels pulled Lot back as the crowd began to beat down the door. Then the angels smote the men with blindness. We're told that they continued all night trying to find the door. In the morning, the angels had to actually carry Lot out of Sodom because they couldn't destroy it until he was gone.

Lot was a type of the church that is to be delivered. Peter tells us that the Lord "delivered just Lot, vexed with the filthy conversation of the wicked: (For that righteous man dwelling among them, in seeing and hearing, vexed his righteous soul from day to day with their unlawful deeds;). The Lord knoweth how to deliver the godly out of temptations, and to reserve the unjust unto the day of judgment to be punished:" (2 Peter 2:7-9). God will deliver the righteous, and He'll also reserve the ungodly for the day of judgment.

The basic principle is that the Lord of the Earth is righteous. He's fair and He won't destroy the righteous with the wicked. When God is the source of the judgment, then God will deliver the righteous out of judgment. Earlier, God judged the world because of its wickedness with the Flood. "And God saw that the wickedness of man was great in the earth, and that every imagination of the thoughts of his heart was only evil continually." (Genesis 6:5). But among all of the unrighteous of the world there was one righteous man, Noah. And God protected and sheltered Noah as His judgment was unleashed. Noah was sealed by God and safely taken through the Flood, just as the One Hundred and Forty Four Thousand in Revelation chapter seven were sealed by God so they would not be harmed by the Tribulation judgments. Noah is a type of the One Hundred and Forty Four Thousand that are sealed and taken through the judgment.

During this same period, there was also one other righteous man, Enoch. "And Enoch walked with God: and he was not; for God took him." (Genesis 5:24). Enoch is an interesting picture of the church. He was translated, or raptured.

I do not believe that the church will go through the Great Tribulation. But there are certain Scriptures that people use to try to show that the church will be there. One argument is based on the interpretation of the 'last trump.' In 1 Corinthians 15, Paul speaks about the Rapture and says, "Behold, I show you a mystery; We shall not all sleep, but we shall all be changed, In a moment, in the twinkling of an eye, at the last trump: for the trumpet shall sound, and the dead shall be raised incorruptible, and we shall be changed." (1 Corinthians 15:51-52). Some try to link this with the seven trumpet judgments of Revelation and say that the seventh trumpet is the last trump. They see this as proof that the Rapture will not take place until the last trump occurs, which is the final judgment.

I see a couple of problems with this. First, the seven trumpet judgments in Revelation are given to the seven angels to sound and to bring in the corresponding judgments upon the earth. When we examine who is blowing each of these trumpets we see that they are all angels. In 1 Thessalonians 4:16, Paul is speaking of the Rapture, "For the Lord himself shall descend from heaven with a shout, with the voice of the archangel, and with the trump of God: and the dead in Christ shall rise first:" (1 Thessalonians 4:16). The trumpet of the Rapture is not that of an angel. It's the trump of God!

After the fourth angel sounds his trump, there's a voice that shouts, "Woe, woe, woe, to the inhabiters of the earth by reason of the other voices of the trumpet of the three angels, which are yet to sound!" (Revelation 8:13). After the fifth trumpet sounds, again the voice says, "One woe is past; and, behold, there come two woes more hereafter." (Revelation 9:12). It's clear that it's a woe that is pronounced to those on the earth. But our being caught up isn't a woe. It's glory!

Another argument that is often given is presented in Revelation chapter 20, as John views the various groups in heaven. Beginning with verse four we read, "And I saw thrones, and they sat upon them, and judgment was given unto them: and I saw the souls of them that were beheaded for the witness of Jesus, and for the word of God, and which had not worshipped the beast, neither his image, neither had received his mark upon their foreheads, or in their hands; and they lived and reigned with Christ a thousand years. But the rest of the dead lived not again until the thousand years were finished. This is the first resurrection." (Revelation 20:4-5). The point they make is that at the first resurrection John sees those who were beheaded for their witness of Jesus, who didn't worship the beast or take the image and receive the mark. They lived and reigned with Christ for a thousand years. Some believe this is solid proof that the church will go through the tribulation and be martyred.

But we need to go back and read it again. In verse four we see thrones, and that to those who sat upon them judgment was given. Let's look back at who these overcomers are. In the message to the overcomers to the church we read, "To him that overcometh will I grant to sit with me in my throne, even as I also overcame, and am set down with my Father in his throne." (Revelation 3:21). John sees the church as a part of the first resurrection. Then he sees those who will be martyred during the Great Tribulation period for their refusal to take the mark of the beast. This is the great number that you find in chapter seven where the elder said, "What are these which are arrayed in white robes? and whence came they? And I said unto him, Sir, thou knowest. And he said to me, These are they which came out of great tribulation, and have washed their robes, and made them white in the blood of the Lamb." (Revelation 7:13-14).

But notice they stand in His holy temple and serve Him day and night continually. The church is the bride of Christ. Jesus said, "Henceforth I call you not servants; for the servant knoweth not what his lord doeth: but I have called you friends; for all things that I have heard of my Father I have made known unto you." (John 15:15). So, we have this second group comprised of the martyred saints during the Great Tribulation period. They will become a part of the kingdom, but the church will have already been raptured. And that's a far better way to go than through martyrdom in the Great Tribulation period!

In Revelation 10:7 we read more about the seventh trumpet. It says, "But in the days of the voice of the seventh angel, when he shall begin to sound, the mystery of God should be finished, as he hath declared to his servants the prophets." (Revelation 10:7). 'Days' is plural, but the Rapture will take place in a moment, in the 'twinkling of an eye.' Therefore, we really can't relate the last trump with the seventh trumpet of Revelation. The seventh trumpet of Revelation will take place over the 'days' of the sounding of the seventh trumpet. In contrast, when the trump of God sounds, we will be changed in a moment.

In Matthew's Gospel, Jesus said, "Immediately after the tribulation of those days shall the sun be darkened, and the moon shall not give her light, and the stars shall fall from heaven, and the powers of the heavens shall be shaken: And then shall appear the sign of the Son of man in heaven: and then shall all the tribes of the earth mourn, and they shall see the Son of man coming in the clouds of heaven with power and great glory. And he shall send his angels with a great sound of a trumpet, and they shall gather together his elect from the four winds, from one end of heaven to the other." (Matthew 24:29-31). We see here that immediately after the tribulation of those days, Jesus appears to the whole world.

Then He gathers together His elect from the four winds, from one end of heaven to the other. But some say, "Isn't the church the elect?" Yes. The church is the elect, but Israel is also the elect. This is a reference to Israel, and you can cross reference it with several passages of the Old Testament where the same thing is declared. God will gather together the Jews from all over the world. In this passage, Jesus is speaking about His elect, the Jewish nation, not the church. Isaiah said, "And he shall set up an ensign for the nations, and shall assemble the outcasts of Israel, and gather together the dispersed of Judah from the four corners of the earth." (Isaiah 11:12). Israel will be regathered.

What about the Scriptures that speak about the Antichrist making war against the saints? Daniel tells us in 7:21, "I beheld, and the same horn (the Antichrist) made war with the saints, and prevailed against them." In Revelation 13:7 we read, "And it was given unto him (the Antichrist) to make war with the saints, and to overcome them: and power was given him over all kindreds, and tongues, and nations." Who are the saints? They can't be the church because Jesus said to Peter, "Upon this rock I will build my church; and the gates of hell shall not prevail against it." (Matthew 16:18). The fact that he makes war on the saints and prevails against them means that they are the Jewish saints, not the church.

I do not believe that the church will see the Antichrist empowered upon the earth. I would not be surprised if the Antichrist is already one of the main figures on the world scene. But I do not believe the church will see the Antichrist display his full power on the earth.

In 2 Thessalonians 2, as Paul is talking about this man of sin, the son of perdition, he declares, "And now ye know what withholdeth that he might be revealed in his time. For the mystery of iniquity doth already work: only he who now letteth will let, until he be taken out of the way. And then shall that Wicked be revealed, whom the Lord shall consume with the spirit of his mouth, and shall destroy with the brightness of his coming:" (2 Thessalonians 2:6-8).

I do not believe that the Antichrist can take over the rule and authority of the earth while the church is still here. I believe that the Holy Spirit within the church is the restraining force that is holding back the powers of darkness from completely engulfing and overwhelming the world right now. But the moment the church is removed, there will be nothing to hinder or hold back the powers of darkness from taking total control. That which restrains shall restrain until he is taken out of the way. Then shall the man of sin, the son of perdition, be revealed. This is the reason why I'm not looking for the Antichrist. This is just another subtle and deceitful device of Satan, that leads people to be looking for the Antichrist rather than looking for Jesus Christ.

The reason some people get their prophetic scenarios confused is because they spiritualize and make the church Israel. They say, *"God is through with the nation of Israel because they rejected the Messiah."* They believe that God has discarded Israel and replaced it with the church, and the church is now *"the Israel of God."* They take those prophecies that refer to Israel as a nation and make them apply to the church. When you do that, it confuses the whole prophetic picture!

If the sun came up this morning, then God's covenant with Israel still stands. He said, "As long as the sun comes up, My covenant with Israel shall stand." God is not through with Israel. In the book of Hosea, God says, "Go back and get her again. Wash her off, clean her up, and take her back." Daniel chapter nine says that God still has a seven-year pact to fulfill with Israel, during which He will deal with them again in a direct way.

You do find the Rapture in type in the Old Testament. Enoch is a type of the church who was translated before the judgment of the flood. Daniel, I believe, is also a type of the church. Remember when Nebuchadnezzar built his great image and demanded that everybody bow down. I believe that this is a type of the image that the Antichrist will build, set in the temple, and demand that everyone worship. Nebuchadnezzar required everyone to bow down to the great image at the sound of the music. So when the music sounded, they all bowed down, with the exception of Shadrach, Meshach, and Abed-nego. The Chaldeans reported to Nebuchadnezzar, "Hey there are three Hebrew boys over here who didn't bow. The music sounded, and they're just standing there!"

So he called in the three Hebrew boys, and said, "What's this I hear? You didn't bow? We'll give you another chance, but if you don't bow you'll be thrown into the burning, fiery furnace!" They said, "King, we're not even careful how we answer you in this matter, because the God that we serve is able to deliver us out of your burning, fiery furnace, and even if He doesn't, we still won't bow!" I love that kind of grit! You don't stop men like that!

Nebuchadnezzar was so angry that he had the furnace heated seven times hotter than it had ever been heated before. The three Hebrews were thrown in and the men that threw them in were burned to death, just because they got close to the fire! But the only thing that burned with Shadrach, Meshach, and Abednego were the ropes by which the Chaldeans bound them. Nebuchadnezzar looked into the furnace and asked, "How many did we throw in there?" They answered, "Three, O king." "But how come I see four? They're walking around in the middle of the fire! And the fourth one looks like the Son of God. Shadrach, Meshach, and Abed-nego, come out of there!"

When they came out, not a hair was singed. There wasn't even the smell of smoke! Everybody was amazed, and Nebuchadnezzar, great at making proclamations, said, "I proclaim there's no God in all the earth like the God of Shadrach, Meshach, and Abed-nego who was able to deliver from the burning, fiery furnace!"

But where was Daniel when this was happening? Do you think Daniel bowed before the image? If you do, you know a different Daniel than I know! Remember back in the first chapter, Daniel had purposed in his heart that he would not defile himself, even with the king's meat. I don't believe that the man who had such purpose of heart would ever bow. Daniel was probably away doing the king's business. Daniel becomes a type of the church which will have been removed when the Antichrist sets up his image and demands everybody to worship. We, the church, will be taking care of business elsewhere, in the heavenly scene!

When you realize that the source of the tribulation is God, it automatically precludes God's people being involved. It wouldn't be just, or consistent, for God to judge the righteous with the wicked.

Peter said that God "spared not the old world, but saved Noah the eighth person, a preacher of righteousness, bringing in the flood upon the world of the ungodly;" (2 Peter 2:5). God spared the righteous but brought the flood upon the world of the ungodly.

That's what the judgment is about. It's targeted at the world of the ungodly. "And turning the cities of Sodom and Gomorrha into ashes condemned them with an overthrow, making them an example unto those that after should live ungodly;" (2 Peter 2:6). But He "delivered just Lot, vexed with the filthy conversation of the wicked: (For that righteous man dwelling among them, in seeing and hearing, vexed his righteous soul from day to day with their unlawful deeds;) The Lord knoweth how to deliver the godly out of temptations, and to reserve the unjust unto the day of judgment to be punished:" (2 Peter 2:7-9). This declares the clear purposes of God.

I believe that through the Old Testament types, such as Lot, Noah, Enoch and Daniel, we see the truth that the church will not be here during the Great Tribulation. Scripture plainly states, "For God hath not appointed us to wrath, but to obtain salvation by our Lord Jesus Christ," (1 Thessalonians 5:9). "Much more then, being now justified by his blood, we shall be saved from wrath through him." (Romans 5:9). And "For the wrath of God is revealed from heaven against all ungodliness and unrighteousness of men, who hold the truth in unrighteousness;" (Romans 1:18)—but this doesn't describe the child of God.

I believe that God wanted every church age to believe that it was the last. Believing this has a three-fold effect. First, it gives us an urgency for the work that we are doing, to get the Gospel out. We don't have much time, so we should "lay aside every weight, and the sin which doth so easily beset us." We need to "run with patience the race that is set before us," (Hebrews 12:1). What we're called to do we need to do quickly. There's an urgency to our work. We need to get the message out because we don't have much time. The Lord is returning soon!

Second, it gives us a correct perspective of material things. The material world is going to burn. We put all of our investments in the things of this material world, but they will all be lost. Jesus said, "But lay up for yourselves treasures in heaven." (Matthew 6:20). He said, "Use the unrighteousness of mammon for eternal purposes." If God does bless you financially, that's great. But we need to use it for eternal purposes. Jesus' imminent return gives us the correct balance between the things of the Spirit and the material things of the world. We recognize that the material world is rapidly passing away and only those things that are eternal will last. Knowing that we have only one life which will soon be past, we recognize that only what we do for Christ will last. This gives us the proper perspective.

The third reason why I'm convinced that Jesus wants every generation to believe it will be the last is that it maintains a purity in our lives. Jesus said, "Blessed is that servant, whom his lord when he cometh shall find so doing." (Matthew 24:46). I don't want the Lord to come and find me watching an X-rated movie or cruising pornographic sites on the Internet. Imagine! Believing that Jesus will return at any time keeps a purity in our lives. The Lord could come today! "Blessed is that servant, whom his lord when he cometh shall find so doing." John said, "Beloved, now are we the sons of God, and it doth not yet appear what we shall be: but we know that, when he shall appear, we shall be like him; for we shall see him as he is. And every man that hath this hope in him purifieth himself, even as he is pure." (1 John 3:2-3). It gives us a purifying hope. That's why I believe it's important that we keep this distinctive of believing in the imminent return of Jesus Christ and not compromise it.

I am looking for the Lord of heaven to come and snatch me away that I might be with Him. As He said,

"Watch ye therefore, and pray always, that ye may be accounted worthy to escape all these things that shall come to pass, and to stand before the Son of man." (Luke 21:36). That is my prayer, and it is my expectation to be there, and the exciting thing is that it could happen at any time! I do believe that the Lord intended us to live in this anticipation in every age of the church.

And I believe that the hope of the glorious appearing of our great God and Savior Jesus Christ is the spark that God has used to bring revival throughout the church. This is what is sparking revival today, the fact that we don't have much time. The Lord is coming soon. We are living at the very edge, and it is as Paul said, "And, that, knowing the time, that now it is high time to awake out of sleep: for now is our salvation nearer than when we believed." (Romans 13:11).

May God help us to maintain that blessed hope and bring it to all people in order that :

1). They might know the urgency of living for Jesus Christ fully and completely;

2). They might have the right priority concerning the things of the world which so easily grasp onto us and hold us back;

3). They might live lives of purity; and

4). They will keep their hearts and lives pure in serving the Lord knowing that He might come at any moment.

I want to be watching and I want to be ready to meet Him when He comes. I don't want to be doing anything that would be dragging me down or holding me back. I want to be ready for my Lord!

I believe it is so important that we proclaim this teaching of the Rapture and keep the people watching and hoping because, without that, what hope do we have in the world today? We need to keep people focused on the truth that a better day is coming very soon. Be ready! The Lord is coming for His people, and He is going to take us to be with Him.

CHAPTER NINE

HAVING BEGUN IN THE SPIRIT

"Not that we are sufficient of ourselves to think any thing as of ourselves; but our sufficiency is of God; Who also hath made us able ministers of the new testament; not of the letter, but of the spirit..."
2 Cor. 3:5-6

Calvary Chapel is a work that was begun by the Spirit. Every new and great movement of God is born of the Spirit. When we examine church history and the various great movements of God, we discover they were all born in the Spirit. Yet such moves of God historically seem to move from that birth in the Spirit to ultimately seeking to be perfected in the flesh. This seems to be a continual cycle in the history of the church. Movements that were once alive in the Spirit become dead in ritualism.

Ritualism is nothing more than a rut, and the only difference between a rut and a grave is the length and the depth. We see the energies of the church expended in life-support systems designed to keep a corpse still gasping for breath. The whole purpose seems to be concentrated in not letting the movement die. We believe that if a program cannot survive on its own, the most merciful thing to do is let it die.

In the Book of Judges we read of the continuing cycle of infidelity on the part of the Israelites. It's almost disgusting to see how the children of Israel did evil in the sight of the Lord, and how the Lord gave them over to their enemies. They would be in bondage, and then, after about forty years, they would cry to the Lord. God would hear them and would send a deliverer, and things would go great for a while. But then, the children of Israel would do evil again in the sight of the Lord, and again they would go into captivity. We see this same cycle in our lives. When things are going great, we have a tendency to slack off. And then when we get into trouble, we cry unto the Lord. Every time I read Judges, I get upset with the children of Israel. I think, "How can you turn your back on the Lord? Can't you see what's going on? Can't you see the cycle that is taking place?"

As I look at church history, I see much the same thing. God raises up a new movement. It's born of the Spirit. There's excitement and revival. There's a powerful moving of the Spirit. Consider some of the modern movements, when God used men like John Wesley and Martin Luther. It is evident that the power and the anointing of the Spirit were on their lives. Yet when we examine the Methodist and Lutheran churches today, with few exceptions, they are laced with modernism. There is a great dearth of the Spirit, even a denying of the power and gifts of the Spirit. But the movements were born of the Spirit. And so goes the history of the church. God raises up a new work and begins a new movement. Calvary Chapel happens to be in the first part of the cycle. The Spirit of God moved, and is moving, and has raised up a new work. It was begun in the Spirit. As the Lord said to Zechariah,

"Not by might, nor by power, but by my spirit, saith the LORD of hosts." (Zechariah 4:6).

Paul wrote to the churches in Galatia, churches begun in the Spirit, and chided them. "Are ye so foolish? Having begun in the Spirit, are ye now made perfect by the flesh?" (Galatians 3:3). God will go to tremendous lengths to make certain that His chosen leaders rely on the Spirit and not on their own power and wisdom. It's interesting to observe the men whom God has used, the men that He has raised up to lead the people in the way of the Lord.

Moses is one example. You remember the story of the burning bush. When God called him, Moses initially objected, saying, "Who am I, that I should go unto Pharaoh, and that I should bring forth the children of Israel out of Egypt?" (Exodus 3:11). Moses said, "Lord, I don't have any confidence. Who am I? I've been out here for forty years." I imagine that he expected to spend the rest of his life simply watching sheep. He figured that was his lot in life. So when the Lord called him, he responded, "Who am I? I don't have any confidence, Lord."

Now, it's interesting that he started out with a lot of confidence, but the Lord knocked it out of him. It's interesting that he had a sense of destiny at one time. Stephen tells us that he thought Israel would understand that God had chosen him to lead them, but they didn't until the second time around (Acts 7). It's a good illustration of the difference between the work of the flesh and the work of the Spirit. Moses first endeavored to do the work of God in the energies of his flesh, but in his own power he couldn't even successfully bury one Egyptian. Yet when he was directed by the Spirit, Israel succeeded in burying the whole army of the Egyptians.

I think most of us can relate to Moses' experience. We so often begin in the flesh to fulfill what we feel the call of God is upon our life. We so often start out in the flesh and find ourselves unsuccessful. I think that when a person fails in the flesh, he often heads for the desert and leaves the ministry, many times never to return. He becomes discouraged and defeated, because he tried in the ability of his flesh to fulfill what he genuinely felt was the call of God upon his heart.

Moses did just that. He felt the call of God upon his heart. He knew that God had ordained him for a purpose, but then he found himself out in the desert for forty years. During this time, he lost his self-worth and the confidence of what God could do through him. He knew that when he had all the cards on his side, he had failed. But God's answer to Moses' objection was, "Certainly I will be with thee;" (Exodus 3:12). To me, that's glorious! "If God be for us, who can be against us?" (Romans 8:31).

Then Moses answered and said, "But, behold, they will not believe me, nor hearken unto my voice: for they will say, The LORD hath not appeared unto thee." (Exodus 4:1). In other words he was saying, "Lord, I don't have credibility. They're not going to believe me. They're just going to say that the Lord hasn't talked to you." God's response to Moses' objection was, "What is in your hand?" He said, "A rod." God said, "Throw it on the ground." And then, through a series of signs, the Lord assured him that He would be with him.

In the tenth verse of chapter four, Moses said unto the Lord, "O my Lord, I am not eloquent, neither heretofore, nor since thou hast spoken unto thy servant: but I am slow of speech, and of a slow tongue." Moses pleaded, "I have no ability. I'm not eloquent. I have slow speech and a slow tongue." To this objection God said, "Who made man's mouth? Who gave you the ability to speak?" God is able to overcome our disabilities. He's the one who created our mouths to begin with.

And then in verse thirteen, he said, "O my Lord, send, I pray thee, by the hand of him whom thou wilt send." In other words, "Lord, get someone else to do the job. I have no desire. I don't want to do it. Just get someone else." Here is where the Lord became upset with Moses and went to an alternate plan. He used Aaron to be Moses' spokesman, but that was God's alternate plan. It's sad, but we often miss God's best and force Him to choose Plan B.

I do believe in a direct will and a permissive will of God. I believe that God will lift us to the highest level that we will allow, and do the best for us on that level. But I also believe that often times we force God to our level rather than being elevated to His. We bring God down in a compromise to our level of commitment.

Look what God had to go through in order to get this man Moses, a man with no confidence, no credibility, no ability, and no desire, yet chosen by God to deliver the people.

In the Book of Judges, when the children of Israel did evil in the sight of the Lord and began to worship false gods, God delivered them into the hands of the Midianites. The Midianites covered the land like grasshoppers. They took the crops as soon as they were ready to harvest. The children of Israel began to cry unto the Lord because of their bondage and misery. So the Lord sent His angel to Gideon who was threshing wheat by a wine press to hide it from the Midianites. The angel of the Lord said to Gideon, "Go in this thy might, and thou shalt save Israel from the hand of the Midianites:" (Judges 6:14). And Gideon responded, "Oh my Lord, wherewith shall I save Israel? Behold, my family is poor in Manasseh, and I am the least in my father's house." (Judges 6:15). "Lord, you're scraping the bottom of the barrel. My family is poor and I'm the least of my family."

He thought he was disqualifying himself, but in reality he was qualifying himself because he was the kind of a person God was looking for. God desired to use a person who knew that he didn't have the capacity or the ability to accomplish the deliverance of a nation, a person who knew he would have to rely upon the Lord if anything was to be done. God also had to bring Moses to this place so that He could use him.

When we don't have confidence in our own power, we know that if the work is going to be done, it has to be done by the Lord. When I felt the call of God on my life to the ministry, I went to Bible College and prepared myself. While in Bible college, I was Senior Class President, Student Body President, and I developed an athletic program for the school. I really felt that I had an awful lot to offer. When I started out in the ministry, I was certain that I had all the qualifications and background to build a successful church anywhere.

I had great confidence, but the Lord put me through the ringer. He allowed me to struggle for seventeen years with no success. I had to work in a secular job in order to support my family so I could stay in the ministry. If it weren't for that sense of the call of God upon my life, I would have given up. In fact, I endeavored to leave the ministry on a couple of occasions, but the Lord brought me back. This all had to happen because of the confidence I had in my own abilities.

The Lord allowed me to spend the prime years of my life failing, until He finally got me to the place where I realized that I really had nothing to offer. Then I began to simply lean on the Spirit and depend upon Him. It was then that I was able to watch God work by His Spirit. I wasn't tempted to take the glory for what God was doing. He brought me to the cross and emptied me of myself and my ambitions. When

God began to work by His Spirit, it became a joyful, thrilling experience just to see what God was able to do.

Many times there is the necessity for this emptying process. When Gideon said, "Lord, my family is one of the poorest in Manasseh, and I am the least in my family," rather than disqualifying himself, he was actually affirming that God had found the kind of a man He was looking for, one who would not take credit or glory for the victories, but would give God the glory.

It's interesting that when God did use Gideon, and the Midianites were scattered and defeated, that they came to Gideon and said, "Rule thou over us... And Gideon said unto them, I will not rule over you, neither shall my son rule over you: the LORD shall rule over you." (Judges 8:22-23). That's the kind of man God was looking for.

I look at the men that God gathered around David. Everyone was in distress, in debt, and discontented. They gathered themselves to him and he became the captain. They were a bunch of malcontents and losers, about 400 men, but God raised these men into a mighty army.

I also look at the men that God gathered around me and I sort of chuckle as I see the ones that God has used. They're much like David's men, sort of the outcasts and cast-offs of society, and yet look what God has done.

When God called Jeremiah, he responded, "Ah, Lord GOD! behold, I cannot speak: for I am a child." (Jeremiah 1:6). When Jesus called His disciples, He chose fishermen and a tax-collector. He didn't go to the Hebrew University in Jerusalem and say, "Now, Gamaliel, who are your sharpest and finest students here?" He went to the Sea of Galilee and called these fishermen.

So Calvary Chapel is not the first time that God has used society's cast-offs to do a wonderful work. But it's interesting and somewhat sad that once God begins to use us, we start looking for reasons why God would use us. We try to become perfected in the flesh.

Writing to the Corinthians Paul said, "For ye see your calling, brethren, how that not many wise men after the flesh, not many mighty, not many noble, are called." (1 Corinthians 1:26). He's calling them to observe that God hasn't called many qualified people—not many wise, after the flesh, not many mighty, not many noble. He goes on to say, "But God hath chosen the foolish things of the world to confound the wise; and God hath chosen the weak things of the world to confound the things which are mighty; And base things of the world, and things which are despised, hath God chosen, yea, and things which are not, to bring to nought things that are:" (1 Corinthians 1:27-28).

He then gives us the reason in 1 Corinthians 1:29, "that no flesh should glory in His presence." The whole purpose of God is to choose those who really aren't qualified, but then to anoint them with His Spirit. Then, when the results are forthcoming, it's an amazement and a wonder to the world. He doesn't desire that any flesh should glory in His presence.

Luke tells us in chapter ten that the disciples returned with excitement over the work of God through their lives. In that hour, while they were talking about it, Jesus was rejoicing in His Spirit. And He said, "I thank thee, O Father, Lord of heaven and earth, that thou hast hid these things from the wise and prudent, and hast revealed them unto babes: even so, Father; for so it seemed good in thy sight." (Luke 10:21). Jesus was thanking the Father that He hid these things from the wise and the prudent and revealed them unto the simple people, because it seemed good in His sight.

It's interesting that having begun in the Spirit, so often, we then seek to be perfected in the flesh. Some of the Calvary Chapel pastors have gone back to school. Some of the schools were quite anxious to have them because of their success in the ministry. They wanted to be able to point to them as having received degrees from their programs, and to be associated with their success in the ministry. The schools were anxious to get them, so they offered them life experience credits.

They were able to take a few courses, and with all their life experience credits get their degrees. Now the schools point to them as classic examples of the success of their graduates. Some of the fellows went back to school to get these degrees because when you're interviewed, they're always asking, *"What degrees do you have?"* and it is kind of embarrassing to say, *"Well I don't have any degree."*

"What seminary did you attend?"

"I didn't attend seminary."

"What university did you attend?"

"Well, I didn't quite make my High School Diploma."

It can be embarrassing to admit that you don't have the educational background. When *"Who's Who"* writes you and says that you've been selected to be in this year's edition, they want to know what degrees you have and what universities you attended because man wants to be able to say, *"Well, look this man has a Ph.D."* Somehow we feel we can be perfected and even prepared in the flesh. We've begun in the Spirit and the only way to have continuing success is to continue in the Spirit.

In Matthew 11:25, "Jesus answered and said, I thank thee, O Father, Lord of heaven and earth, because thou hast hid these things from the wise and prudent, and hast revealed them unto babes." It's interesting how we try to disqualify ourselves from the revelation of God's truths by becoming wise and prudent. Jesus was rejoicing that His Father didn't reveal these truths unto the wise and prudent, but unto babes so that the glory might go to God.

When Gideon was ready to go out against the Midianites, he was greatly outnumbered. There were at least 135,000 Midianites and he had only 32,000 men who mustered to the first call. But God said, "The people that are with thee are too many for me to give the Midianites into their hands, lest Israel vaunt themselves against me, saying, Mine own hand hath saved me." (Judges 7:2). The Lord is saying that He can't do it with the 32,000. You see God wants to work, but God wants the glory for the work that He does. That's why He uses the simple things of this world in order to confound the wise. People can only look on, shake their heads, and say, "I don't understand it, but God's anointing is there. God is sure using them." I wonder how many times the work that God wants to do is hindered because God can't find simple men. All He has is a bunch of Ph.D.s out here.

Now, I've been accused of being anti-intellectual. Even Calvary Chapel is often branded as anti-intellectual. I suppose I am guilty, but I don't apologize for it. I do believe in education. My own life has been a life of study. The Scripture tells us to "Study to shew thyself approved unto God, a workman that needeth not to be ashamed, rightly dividing the word of truth." (2 Timothy 2:15). I believe that God uses human instruments, and that He prepares the instruments that He uses. I believe that it's important to be prepared in the Word of God, but not from a purely natural humanistic standpoint. True education doesn't come from the wisdom of the world, but by the guidance and the wisdom that comes from the Holy Spirit.

When the disciples stood before the religious council, the council marveled at their understanding of the Scripture. They observed that they had been with Jesus. Likewise, when we spend time with Jesus in His Word, we'll get all we need to prepare us for service and for ministry. You don't need four years of seminary and a Ph.D. Many times they can be a greater hindrance than a blessing. I believe that the title *'Doctor'* puts a wall between you and the people, which makes you less effective in ministering to them. People will put you on a pedestal the moment that they say, *'Doctor.'* You put yourself in an element above them, and they feel inferior. Then you end up not really ministering to them on a level that they can relate to.

Once a year we have a Pastors' Planning Meeting for our annual Pastors' Conference. I get together with Raul Ries, Mike MacIntosh, Greg Laurie, Skip Heitzig, and several others. At the session we had after Raul and Mike got their doctoral degrees, everyone was sort of joshing them about their titles. *'Dr. Raul Ries'* and *'Dr. Mike MacIntosh.'* We were giving them a bad time, and one of the fellows remarked, *"Well, if you guys can just go to school and get enough education, you can probably reduce your churches to manageable sizes."*

I thought that was classic. Because having begun in the Spirit, if you're going to try to be made perfect in the flesh, you're only going to hinder what God has done and wants to do. The only way is to continue in the Spirit. **Having begun in the Spirit, let us continue in the Spirit!** Thank God that Raul is still Raul, and Mike is still Mike, men who know their own limitations and inabilities, men who still rely wholly on the Spirit.

The Lord said to Jeremiah, "Let not the wise man glory in his wisdom, neither let the mighty man glory in his might, let not the rich man glory in his riches: But let him that glorieth glory in this, that he understandeth and knoweth me," (Jeremiah 9:23-24). That's the only thing that's worthwhile, that you understand and know God. "I am the LORD which exercise lovingkindness, judgment, and righteousness, in the earth: for in these things I delight, saith the LORD." (Jeremiah 9:24).

That's why God chooses such totally unqualified people like us, fills us with His Spirit, and then does a mighty work through us that astounds and baffles the world. Now, how can we be so foolish as to try to find some reason in us to explain why God used us so that we might glory in ourselves rather than glorying in the Lord and in what He has done?

Paul writing to the Corinthians said, "For who maketh thee to differ from another? and what hast thou that thou didst not receive? now if thou didst receive it, why dost thou glory, as if thou hadst not received it?" (1 Corinthians 4:7). So what do you have more than anybody else? Whatever you have, you've received it as a gift from God. If you have received it, then why do you glory as though you didn't, as though you are something special?

CHAPTER TEN

THE SUPREMACY OF LOVE

"By this shall all men know that ye are my disciples, if ye have love one to another."
John 13:35

Without love all the gifts and powers of the Holy Spirit are meaningless and worthless. "Though I speak with the tongues of men and of angels, and have not charity, I am become as sounding brass, or a tinkling cymbal." (1 Corinthians 13:1). Paul says that there are those who place a heavy emphasis on speaking in tongues, and who look at that gift as the primary evidence of the infilling or baptism of the Spirit. But if those same people don't have love, speaking in tongues is no more meaningful than a noise made by hitting a cymbal or triangle. It's just a noise. It's not proof or evidence of anything. It may be held up as a primary evidence of the presence of the Spirit, but it doesn't evidence anything if there's no love. It's the same as a sounding brass or a tinkling cymbal. It's just a noise, but not real proof.

All our doctrinal orthodoxy and understanding of the Scriptures are of no value without love. Though I understand the great mysteries, things like the mystery of the Godhead, the sovereignty of God, or the responsibility of man, if I don't have love, they're worthless. If I'm just getting in people's faces and working to make them see and believe my side, my doctrinal purity profits me nothing. It's all worthless without love.

I've come to the conclusion that it's more important that I have the right attitude than that I have the right answers. If my answers are wrong, God can change them in a moment by the revelation of His truth. But often times it takes a whole lifetime to change an attitude. Better that we have the right attitude and the wrong answers, than the right answers and the wrong attitude. Remember that the next time you get into an argument with someone over some doctrinal position or issue.

God's supreme desire for us is that we experience His love and then share that love with others. Jesus said, "A new commandment I give unto you, That ye love one another; as I have loved you, that ye also love one another." (John 13:34). That's a big order. He then said, "He that hath my commandments, and keepeth them, he it is that loveth me: and he that loveth me shall be loved of my Father, and I will love him, and will manifest myself to him." (John 14:21). John said, "If a man say, I love God, and hateth his brother, he is a liar: for he that loveth not his brother whom he hath seen, how can he love God whom he hath not seen?" (1 John 4:20). And he questions, "How dwelleth the love of God in him?" (1 John 3:17).

John speaks quite a bit about keeping God's commandments in his first epistle. But what is the commandment that we have heard of Him? It's that we should love one another.

As we minister to a fellowship or a group, whether it's a home Bible study or a church of ten thousand people, we need to make certain that one of our major themes is love. That love needs to be demonstrated by our own actions, attitudes, and life. May everyone see the love of Christ manifested in us. As Paul said to Timothy. "Be thou an example of the believers, in word, in conversation, in charity, in spirit, in faith, in purity." (1 Timothy 4:12). Constantly seek to be understanding and compassionate, seeing people in and through the compassion of Jesus Christ.

I've found that the key to compassion is understanding. Ezekiel once said, "I sat where they sat," (Ezekiel 3:15). I believe that's a very good thing to try to do, at least in your own mind. Put yourself in the other man's shoes. Put yourself in his life situation. Sit where he's sitting. See it from his side. We're always seeing things only from our side, but try and look at it from his side.

Sometimes there are people who irritate us because of their mannerisms or because of certain characteristics that are distasteful to us. I heard Dr. James Dobson once say that there was a fellow in school that he absolutely hated, and that this guy also hated him. All through school they just couldn't stand each other. Some time later Dr. Dobson met the fellow at a convention, and he knew he was going to have to face him. So, he wrote down the things that irritated him and that he disliked about the guy. Then when he met the guy he said, "You know I have to confess to you that all through school I hated you, and these are the reasons why." Then he started reading off all the reasons why he hated the guy. The fellow responded by saying, "Well, I hated you, too, and for the very same reasons!" Dr. Dobson said that he looked at his reasons again and realized he was looking in a mirror. I find this to be very true, and yet quite amusing.

Those traits we dislike about ourselves are the same ones that we absolutely abhor in others. We've come to tolerate and live with them in ourselves, but when we see them in others, we can't stand them. They're irritating and they upset us. Understanding is such an important component of compassion.

For years I would spend my vacations directing youth camps. It's one of my favorite experiences in life. They were the most glorious times I could ever hope for. My family would go, too, and they would have the opportunity of being able to enjoy the glorious countryside. Kay used to say, "But, honey, you didn't get a vacation." And I would say, "Oh, yes I did."

Now in directing youth camps you'll find there are those irritable little guys that if you say, "Sit down," they will stand up. If you say, "Stand up," they'll stay seated. If you say, "Now we don't throw rocks at trees. It can nick the bark, and the beetles can get in, so we don't throw rocks at trees," you'll invariably catch these types throwing rocks at trees. They are always in rebellion. I have had counselors come to me and say, "Chuck, you better move this kid to another counselor because I won't be responsible for what I do to him. I am going to kill him. I can't stand him."

So I would say, "Send him to me." Of course, they'd grab the kid by the nape of the neck and march him in and say, "This is the one I was telling you about." I would sit him down and give him one of my smiles, and I'd say, "What do you want to drink, coke, seven-up, orange soda, or what?" I would go over to the snack shop and get him a drink and his favorite candy bar. When he's first sitting there, he's in rebellion thinking he isn't going to tell me anything. So I start breaking down his defenses. It's amazing how a candy bar and the sugar in his system will break down his defenses. I start to break down that wall that he has built up and

I begin to show interest in him. The dialogue usually went a little bit like this:

"Well, where are you from?"

"Black Canyon."

"Where is Black Canyon? Is that by the Verde River?"

"Yeah."

"Great. Are you in school?"

"Yeah."

"Well, tell me a little bit about your family. Where is your dad?"

"I don't have a dad."

"Oh, what happened?"

"I don't know. I've never had a dad."

"Hmm, that must be hard."

As you begin to dig, you find out that his mom works in a bar and has a different man home every night, and the kid is left on his own. The men that come home are not friendly to him, and he's learned to just stay out of the way. His mom really isn't interested in him, either. As the story begins to unfold, your heart just goes out in compassion. This poor little kid doesn't have a chance. He's built up all of this resentment and all of this hatred against the world that he has to live in. He's learned to build up these walls. He doesn't dare let anybody get close to him. He has to protect himself. He's the only one looking out for himself. Now you have understanding. You realize why he's responding and reacting the way he is.

Then I would go back to the counselor, sit down with him, and share what's going on in this little kid's life. I wanted to give the counselor an understanding so that he'd have compassion. I would often advise the counselor to make him his helper and keep the boy close to him, to give him some responsibilities and show him loads of attention, and to give him a lot of support. It's amazing the changes that can develop in just a week's time with compassion.

As a pastor, you're going to have people in your congregation that you'll feel the same way about. You'd like to kill them. But you need to have understanding. Get to know them. Get to understand where the thorn is, what's irritating them. If you seek to understand them, then as you have compassion, you can truly minister to them. You can't truly minister to anyone you don't feel compassion toward. How many times do you read in the Scriptures, "And Jesus was moved with compassion," when He saw the needs of the people? He understood the need. He didn't need someone to testify to Him because He knew what was in man. It was because He had compassion. So, seek to understand.

Jesus said to His disciples, "Ye have not chosen me, but I have chosen you, and ordained you, that ye should go and bring forth fruit, and that your fruit should remain:" (John 15:16). The fruit of the Spirit is love. He has chosen you to bring forth this fruit. In John 13:34, right after He told the disciples to love one another even as He has loved us, He goes on to say, "Herein is my Father glorified, that ye bear much fruit; so shall ye be my disciples. As the Father hath loved me, so have I loved you: continue ye in my love." (John 15:8-9). So we can vividly see the supremacy of love.

CHAPTER ELEVEN

STRIKING THE BALANCE

"Study to shew thyself approved unto God, a workman that needeth not to be ashamed, rightly dividing the word of truth."
2 Tim. 2:15

An important characteristic of Calvary Chapel Fellowships is our desire not to divide God's people over non-essential issues. This is not to say that we do not have strong convictions. When the Bible speaks clearly, we must as well. But on other issues we try to recognize the Scriptural validity of both sides of a debate and avoid excluding or favoring those in one camp over the other.

An example of this kind of inclusiveness is found in our approach to the debatable issue concerning the ministry of the Holy Spirit. We don't take a typical Pentecostal view, nor do we take a typical Baptist view. The minute you set your position one way or the other, you've lost half of your congregation. Why would you want to lose half your congregation? Our desire is to be able to minister to as broad a group of people as possible. The minute we start taking hard-line positions on any of the non-foundational controversial issues, we alienate part of the people. In the essential doctrines of the faith, we must take a firm stand. But in the non-essential areas, we accept that people may have differing views, and we accept these in the spirit of grace. It's important to recognize that we can agree to disagree and still maintain a spirit of unity and love.

We do believe in the validity of the gifts of the Spirit, and that these gifts can be expressed today. But we don't believe in excesses that so often accompany a freedom in the use of the gifts of the Spirit. So we avoid the controversy.

If people want to speak in tongues, we encourage them to do so in a private devotional setting to assist in communicating their love, their praises, and their prayers to God. We look to 1 Corinthians 14 as our biblical example. We don't insist that a person speak in tongues as the primary evidence of the baptism of the Holy Spirit. We believe that there are other evidences that are more credible than speaking in tongues. As Paul said, "Though I speak with the tongues of men and of angels, and have not charity, I am become as sounding brass, or a tinkling cymbal." (1 Corinthians 13:1). We don't emphasize tongues as the primary manifestation of the baptism of the Holy Spirit, but we look for love as the fruit of the Spirit. I believe that we can stand on a solid Scriptural basis doing that and, at the same time, encourage people to receive the gifts of tongues.

As Paul explained, you may use it for your personal prayer life and for your devotional life, singing unto the Lord. "For if I pray in an unknown tongue, my spirit prayeth, but my understanding is unfruitful. What is it then? I will pray with the spirit, and I will pray with the understanding also: I will sing with the spirit, and I will sing with the understanding also. Else when thou shalt bless with the spirit, how shall he that occupieth the room of the unlearned say Amen at thy giving of thanks, seeing he understandeth not what thou sayest?" (1 Corinthians 14:14-16). If you're in a public assembly with no interpreter present, and someone is speaking in tongues, how is a person sitting in the seat of the unlearned going to understand? You might well be praising God, but the other people aren't edified. We need to do all things decently and in order. In this area, we don't fit in the Pentecostal category, nor do we fit in the cessionist category that would deny any valid experience of the sign gifts of the Holy Spirit today.

Another example of maintaining a balance on debatable issues is our approach to Calvinism. This is an area that people get very emotional about. We're neither 'Five Point Calvinists', nor are we Arminian. We do believe in the security of the believer. We don't believe that you can lose your salvation because you lost your temper or told a lie and, as a result, need to go forward next Sunday night to repent and get resaved.

We believe in the security of the believer but we also believe in the 'perseverance of the saints.' We don't believe that because you are a saint you will necessarily persevere, but that you need to persevere because you're a saint. Jesus said, "If ye continue in my word, then are ye my disciples indeed;" (John 8:31), and "If a man **abide not** in me, he is cast forth as a branch, and is withered; and men gather them, and cast them into the fire, and they are burned. **If ye abide in me**, and my words abide in you, ye shall ask what ye will, and it shall be done unto you." (John 15:6-7). Jesus Himself is the One that brought up the possibility of a person not abiding in Him. So we seek to take a balanced position rather than getting on one side and pressing the 'Five Points of Calvinism.' When you take hard stands on these non-foundational issues, you'll just empty your church of all of those who have

Methodist, Nazarene, and other Arminian-influenced backgrounds. Why would you want to do that?

The eternal security of the believer is a debatable issue at best. There are Scriptures on both sides. You have John 3:16. What does "Whosoever believeth in Him" mean? Does that mean that anybody can be saved? It appears to me to mean that, and so we don't take the hard-line Calvinistic position of limited atonement that says Jesus didn't die for everybody, only those who would believe in Him. We do not accept that believing in Him has nothing to do with human responsibility, but is totally the sovereign choice of God. This position states that God has ordained some to be saved and some to be lost. If God has ordained you to be lost, tough luck, buddy. There's nothing we can do. This is a denial of the free moral agency. Instead, we believe that God has given us the capacity of choice. The reason He gave us a capacity of choice is so that the love we express toward Him might be meaningful and real. That's the balanced position that we take.

There are people who are always trying to pigeon-hole Calvary Chapel. Do you believe in eternal security? I say, "Yes, of course I believe in eternal security. As long as I abide in Christ, I'm eternally secure." Now, dispute that. If you don't abide in Christ, are you secure? Can you have security outside of Jesus Christ? I don't know of any security outside of Jesus Christ. But I believe as long as I abide in Him, He's going to keep me from falling, He's going to present me faultless before the presence of His glory with exceeding joy. And no man can pluck me out of His hand. I believe that, and I experience God's security.

So often these issues come down to a matter of semantics. People end up dividing over the interpretation of a few words. We had a staff member here at Calvary who was very much committed to support groups. During his time with us he led many to faith in Christ. Unfortunately, we had a parting of the ways that left this man so bitter that he now belongs to a group called "Fundamentalists Anonymous." He is now actively encouraging people to abandon a biblically based faith in Jesus Christ.

Is he saved? In reality, he's an enemy of Christ. If I were an Arminian, I'd say he's backslidden. If I were describing him from a Calvinist position, I would say he was never saved. Now we're both describing the same man, but the terms by which we describe him create the division.

We recognize this fact. The man has turned his back on Jesus Christ. It's obvious. Is he backslidden, or was he ever saved? The problem is if I say he was never saved, then where's my security? How do I know I'm saved? He had the earmarks of being saved. He had a desire to serve the Lord. He was seeking to lead others to Jesus Christ. I desire to serve the Lord and I desire to lead others to Jesus Christ. So maybe I'm not saved. Now, that isn't security to me.

So, you see, it's a matter of semantics. How can we describe what we observe in a person's relationship with the Lord? The whole division is over whether I describe him as backslidden, or whether I just say he was never saved. If we divide, we naturally create a division. We drive half the people out of the church because I'm going to say he's backslidden and the next guy is going to say he was never saved. When we allow this kind of debate we divide the church.

That's why I don't take a dogmatic position on this because I believe that the Scripture teaches both the sovereignty of God and the responsibility of man. If you take either of these positions to an extreme, to the denying of the other, then you've got a real problem because the Scriptures teach both. But then you might ask, "How can we reconcile them?" I don't. I don't have to. God didn't ask me to. God just asked me to believe. When I come across a person living in fornication, in adultery, or walking after the flesh and he says, "Don't worry about me, man! I accepted Christ at a Billy Graham crusade when I was a kid." Yet the person is a drunkard and fornicator. But he says, "Once I've been saved I'm always saved! So don't worry about me." Believe me, I'm going to rattle that guy's cage as best I can. I'm going to take him to Galatians 5 where the Bible talks about the works of the flesh. At the end of that listing the Bible declares, "As I have also told you in time past, that they which do such things shall not inherit the kingdom of God." (Galatians 5:21). I'll take him to Corinthians and to Ephesians. I'll show him where those who are living after the flesh and devoted to living after the fallen nature's desires, are not going to inherit the kingdom of God.

Yet, on the other hand, if I'm speaking to saints with an oversensitive conscience who, every time they mess up and do something wrong, feel that they've lost their salvation, I'm going to take them to the Scriptures that give us the assurance of God's love. I'll show them how Christ is holding them and that no man can pluck them out of the Father's hand. I'm going to take them to the passages that will give them assurance.

So the position I take on the issue all depends on the condition of the person I'm talking to. I can take either side and argue it ad infinitum. I can trade Scriptures with people on both sides of the issue. I can let you choose what side you want, and I'll take the other side. I can produce as many Scriptures and make as good an argument as you can.

So the very fact that it is an argumentative issue demonstrates that there are two sides. If there was a clear definitive teaching, then there would be no argument. If we didn't have Scriptures that declare,

"Come! And let him that is athirst come. And whosoever will, let him take the water of life freely," (Revelation 22:17), then you'd have no argument. But the fact is that there is the clear teaching of choice given to us by God. He expects us to make that choice. "Choose you this day whom ye will serve," (Joshua 24:15). "How long halt ye between two opinions? if the LORD be God, follow him: but if Baal, then follow him." (1 Kings 18:21). But yet Jesus said to His disciples, "Ye have not chosen me, but I have chosen you, and ordained you, that ye should go and bring forth fruit, and that your fruit should remain:" (John 15:16). There are two sides to this issue, and it's important that we not get caught in a hard-line position on one side to the exclusion of the other, because then you've effectively divided your congregation.

I, like every other student in Bible college, wrestled with this issue. I was reading Arthur W. Pink's *The Sovereignty of God.* I got so confused because Pink states that man has no choice in the issue of salvation. It is all up to God. There's no human responsibility. As I was reading the book, I got so confused that I finally stood up, took the paperback, and threw it across the room. I felt like Martin Luther throwing an ink well at the devil. I said, "God, I can't understand it." I was frustrated mentally. It was then that the Lord spoke to my heart and said, "I didn't ask you to understand it, I only asked you to believe My Word."

I rested from that point on. I still cannot in my mind rationalize the two positions. I can't bring the two together, which is the problem that we so often have. It's like a railroad track. The two rails are running parallel and if they come together you're in trouble. So I believe them both, even though I'm not able to reconcile them in my mind. But I don't have to anymore. I can be satisfied just to believe them without having to reduce them to the narrow limits of my intellect.

Trying to bring God within the confines of my intellect is a real lesson in frustration. Try to understand eternity! Try to understand infinity! Try to understand the limitlessness of space! Try to imagine where the edge of space is. How far do you have to go out before you see the sign that says, *"Dead end. No exit. Nothing beyond this point"*? We need to recognize that God is greater than what can be confined or understood in our mind. He said, "For my thoughts are not your thoughts, neither are your ways my ways, saith the LORD. For as the heavens are higher than the earth, so are my ways higher than your ways, and my thoughts than your thoughts." (Isaiah 55:8-9). Now if God says that His ways are beyond our finding out, then it's an exercise in futility to try to find out. It's beyond our finding out.

We need to just accept the limitlessness of God. When I come to these crisis points now, those places where my intellect starts to hit a dead end, I simply stand there and worship the God Who is so awesome that I can't reduce Him to my understanding.

As you begin to minister, as you go through the Word, you will come across those Scriptures that speak of the sovereignty of God. When you do, teach it. When you come across those Scriptures that teach the responsibility of man, then teach that. In this way, you can be sure that the people are getting a well-balanced spiritual diet.

CHAPTER TWELVE

VENTURES OF FAITH

"But without faith it is impossible to please him: for he that cometh to God must believe that he is, and that he is a rewarder of them that diligently seek him."
Heb. 11:6

It's always an exciting thing to give God a chance to work. God wants you to be a part of what He is doing. God doesn't want to stop working, so it's important for us to discover what He wants to do. I have found that the way we discover how God wants to work is to venture out in faith. We need to step out and see what the Lord might do. But, as we step out in faith, there has to be a guard against presumption. A lot of people who test the waters to see what God might want to do make a serious mistake by falling back on human effort when God's hand obviously is not in it. Sometimes we can get so committed to something that our reputation seems to be on the line. Then we start pumping extra energy and effort into a program that wasn't of God to begin with.

I've ventured out many times only to discover that God wasn't in it. What do you do then? You retreat. What gets us into trouble is when we proudly say, "We're going to make this thing succeed." We find ourselves spending all of our energy trying to create something that God isn't a part of, and it can just rip you up. When I step out in faith, if it succeeds, I rejoice and say, "Great! The Lord led me." If it doesn't succeed, I step back and say, "I thought it was a good idea, but it sure fell on its nose." So, I think that there are certain precautions that one must take in any venture in faith.

In the Old Testament, we have the story of Saul. During the time of his reign he established a standing army. He was commander over the larger part, and Jonathan was over the lesser part. It wasn't a big army, but the Philistines had invaded the land and were determined this time to completely wipe out Israel. They had amassed large forces of troops and chariots. They were such an awesome military threat that most of the Israeli army deserted and fled to the other side of the Jordan River. There were just a few men left, and they were fearful. Then Jonathan woke up one night with what must have been either a troubling thought, or an exciting thought. If God wants to deliver the Philistines to Israel, He doesn't need the whole army. If God wants to work, He can work with one man as easily as one hundred thousand men.

Now, when you stop to think about that from a logical standpoint, it's really true. God doesn't need a whole army. All God needs is one person in harmony with His purpose. God can accomplish His desires through one man. All He needs is just one man. That's both a challenging and exciting thought. That thought kept Jonathan awake until he finally woke up his armor bearer and said, "Let's go over and see if God wants to deliver the Philistines to Israel today."

So, they took a venture in faith. It's having a mindset that says, "Let's see if God wants to work today. Let's see what God might want to do today." It's simply making yourself available. But Jonathan did set up a safeguard. As they were on their way over to the Philistine camp, he said, "We have to make sure God is in this. So when we're spotted by their sentries, if they say to us, 'Hey, you guys! What are you doing here? Wait, we're going to come down and teach you a lesson.' Then we'll know that God doesn't want to deliver the Philistines today. But if they say, 'Hey, you guys! Come up here and we'll show you a thing or two, then we'll know that God does want them into our hands."

So they left the matter open. They didn't presumptuously tear into the Philistines because they thought, "God is going to be with us and we're going to wipe them out." There was a certain amount of precaution. If I don't know for sure, a little precaution is always wise. The Bible is full of stories of people who ventured out in faith, giving God an opportunity to do what He intended to do, simply by making themselves available to Him.

Several years ago, we heard that the radio station KWVE was up for sale. At that time we were being broadcast on KYMS. We were actually providing them with the financial funding and visibility needed to get them started. The station president had bought the station in order to bring Christian radio to Orange County. *The Word For Today* was originally the station's anchor program. But when new ownership took over, they decided to go to a contemporary music format and cut off the Bible teaching programs. So we went on KBRT, but they were extremely expensive.

Then we heard that KWVE was up for sale. We decided, "Let's just make them an offer, and see what the Lord will do. If the Lord wants us to have it, they'll accept the offer and the thing will work out." We gave

God a chance to work. We asked God, "Do you want a radio station in Orange County that will broadcast worship music and Bible teaching? Do you desire that?"

There we were, willing to venture out and give God a chance. It was solely an act of faith. We were determined that we weren't going to dicker and negotiate. We were just going to give them a figure. Then they said, "We have others interested, too." And we said, "Fine." High pressure sales tactics won't work when you're committed to the Lord. We prayed, "Well, Lord if you want it, fine, and if not, that's fine too." Finally, it worked out that they accepted the offer and so we have KWVE today, and it's providing a glorious ministry. Interestingly it is also showing a profit, and yet we charge one third the cost of broadcasting on other religious stations in the area. We can air our ministry partners' programs for a lot less, and give them a good audience. God has blessed KWVE, but it's because we stepped out and said, "God, if this is what you want, we will take the step in faith and make the offer."

But there was also a TV station that came up for sale. We put in an offer on it. We saw it as an opportunity for the Lord to televise what we call "Representative Christianity", instead of the lunatic fringe programming that was so prevalent. Our bid wasn't accepted so we just walked away from it. We didn't push and we didn't get ahead of the Lord. If God wanted us to have it, He would have made it available, and, if not, we weren't going to strive or negotiate. So, stepping out in faith and seeing what God wants to do is what you might call, "testing the waters."

A few years ago we realized that we needed a larger facility for our Bible College, which was located at Twin Peaks Conference Center at the time. Twin Peaks needed the entire conference center to house the school, so we weren't able to continue our regular conferences along with the Bible School. Then a large, beautiful ranch property owned by the Los Angeles Rescue Mission became available in Vista.

We put a deposit on it, but many members of the Vista City Council living near the property started a media drive against us. We decided, "We don't have to fight this", and we backed away from the deal. A realtor, who saw the notice in the paper that we had cancelled the escrow, called us, and said that he happened to have a listing in Murrieta Hot Springs, which had not yet been made public. We went and looked at the property, and we could see the potential there. We made our "low ball" offer on it and said, "If the Lord's in it, we'll get it." And we got it!

The interesting thing, though, is that we'd been wanting the facility next door to Calvary Chapel Costa Mesa for many years. This six-story office building was originally offered to us for $18 million. A few years ago we made an offer of $10 million and they said, "No, it's worth more than that." Then a person came forward and put together a deal with the major tenant. The property was then offered to us for $8.9 million. We went ahead and got it for $1 million less than we offered! We really saw the hand of the Lord in that.

But the interesting thing is that if we had bought the building next door first, we would never have purchased Murrieta Hot Springs. We wouldn't have been in the position to buy Murrieta. So we can see the hand of God in the whole process. He wanted us to have both of these properties, and He orchestrated the timing in such a way that we were already into Murrieta when the office building became available at a price that was too good to pass up. So here we are now with both pieces of property.

We were taking baby steps, and the Lord wanted us to take a giant step. You just keep going forward, and as long as the Lord opens the door, you just keep moving ahead. There is always a sense of daring in a step of faith. You dare to step out to see what the Lord might want to do. But, again, if God isn't in it, we don't fight Him. We don't press. We don't manipulate. We don't force things. If God's in it, it's going to go His way. It's going to go smoothly, and we're not going to have to make compromises.

When Greg Laurie took over our Monday Night Bible Study, God began to really bless him and the ministry. We saw young people coming forward every Monday night to receive Christ. I called Greg in and said, "Greg, why don't we see if we can get a week this summer at Pacific Amphitheater. Let's get a larger facility to see what God might do if we had more room. We're overflowing the place on Monday night and we don't have room for everybody. So, why don't we try Pacific Amphitheater?"

That was in April, and Greg didn't think that we had enough time to do it. He said, "You can't do it now!" And I said, "Why not? Let's see if they have a week available. Let's just see what God might want to do with a larger venue."

We called Pacific Amphitheater and they did have a week available in the summer. We decided to call the event "Harvest Crusades." We were absolutely overjoyed because that week was so glorious! The last night they actually had to lock the gates because there were so many people inside. They set up loud speakers outside so the people who couldn't get in could hear. It was a thrill! And it's just grown and developed from there, but it began with only a simple step of faith. "Let's see what God might want to do. Let's give God a chance to work. Let's step out." We might risk a few dollars, but, as the saying goes, "nothing ventured, nothing gained."

Another classic Old Testament example of stepping out in faith took place when the city of Samaria was being besieged by the Syrians. The conditions had become so bad in the city of Samaria that they were selling the jaw bone of a donkey for sixty-five pieces of silver and a quarter of a cab of dove's dung for five pieces of silver. The women had turned to cannibalism. One woman cried out to the king pleading for help, but he answered, "How can I help you? I don't have food on my own table." She said, "This woman and I made an arrangement to eat our babies, and we boiled my baby and ate it, and now she has hid her baby. So make her produce it so we can eat it." The king tore his clothes and said, "God help me if I don't get the head of that prophet, Elisha!" He was blaming God for his own problems. (2 Kings 6:24-33).

Elisha was an interesting kind of a prophet, as well as an interesting man. He had amazing spiritual insight and such a close communion with God that he was surprised when God didn't show him things. Now, every once in a while God has shown me something, but I'm always shocked and surprised when He does. I get excited! It happens only a few times in your life. But Elisha was so tuned in that he was surprised when God didn't show him things. I'm surprised when God does, but he was surprised when God didn't.

Elisha was in his house with his friends when he started talking to himself, "Hmm, wow! Can you beat that." So his friends asked, "What's going on, Elisha?" And he replied, "The king is sending a guy down here to get my head. So, when he knocks on the door, you guys open it and pin him with the door. For, behold! The feet of his master are right behind him." Pretty soon there was a knock on the door. Elisha's friends opened the door, pinned the guy against the door, and held him there. Then the king came riding up with the prime minister and said, "I finally got you! You've troubled Israel long enough." Elisha replied, "I'm not the one who has troubled Israel. You're the one that's troubled Israel by bringing in the worship of Baal. You're the one to blame!"

He went on to say, "Don't worry. Tomorrow by this time, they will be selling a bushel of fine flour in the gates of Samaria for sixty-five cents." The prime minister scoffed at the promise of God saying, "Behold, if the LORD would make windows in heaven, might this thing be?" (2 Kings 7:2). And Elisha said, "Behold, thou shalt see it with thine eyes, but shalt not eat thereof." (2 Kings 7:19).

Why did the prime minister stagger at the promises of God? Because he tried to figure out, in a human way, how God could do it. Many times, that's when we get into trouble. We can't see how God could do it. We've tried everything and we've plotted every way and we've just had to conclude that it's impossible. We're prone, just like the prime minister, to say, "If God should open windows of heaven, could such a thing be?" Elisha said, "You'll see it, but you won't eat it." God's going to do His work, but because of your unbelief, you won't be able to benefit or profit from the work of God.

The story continues with four leprous men who lived in the garbage heap outside of the city of Samaria. Because of their leprosy, they weren't allowed to enter the city. They existed on the garbage thrown over the wall, but because of the famine in the city they were starving. One of them looked at the others and said, "Why sit we here until we die?" (2 Kings 7:3). "There's no sense in going into the city. So let's go over to the camp of the Syrians. Who can tell, maybe they will have mercy on us and give us a crust of bread that we might live, or maybe they will kill us. But so what? We're going to die anyway." They began a venture in faith that was premised on the sliver of a hope that maybe they would be given a crust of bread, or maybe they wouldn't.

I'm amazed that many churches don't come to this same place, as the few people left look around at each other. I'm surprised they don't say, "Well, why do we just sit here until we die? Let's do something. Maybe it will work, and maybe it won't, but if it doesn't, it doesn't matter, because we're dying anyhow. Let's venture out."

I think of all of the ventures of faith that have been made throughout history on just that kind of a premise. Who knows what God might be wanting to do? Let's step out. Let's find out. Let's give God a chance. The story of Elisha concludes when the Syrians heard noises that they interpreted as the chariots of Egypt. They figured that the king had hired the Egyptians as mercenaries, and panic broke out. They began to flee, and by the time the four lepers came to the first tent, they found that supper was on the table, but no one was there to eat it. So they ate and grabbed all the treasures. They went to the next tent and found the same thing. It was empty of men, but filled with food.

As they were trying to grab the loot, bury it and hide it, one of them said, "Hey, fellows! We'd better let them know in town what God has done. If we just hide this and hoard it for ourselves, mischief will come to us." When they returned to the city, they cried to the guard on the wall, "The camp of the Syrians is empty. There's plenty of food for everybody. Let the king know that people don't need to go to sleep hungry tonight." When the report came to the king, he said, "It's a trap. Those clever Syrians know how hungry we are, so they pulled back into the shadows to wait for us to come pouring out of the city. Then they're going to pounce on us and kill us. Don't let anybody out of the gates of the city. Keep the city gates barred."

I think of the tragedy and the cost of unbelief. It keeps us from partaking even when God has provided abundantly. I have met people that have that kind of mentality. They always say that it's a trap of some kind. It's too good to be true and there has to be a hitch to it. When God is working, they're afraid to venture in.

There's a passage of Scripture that has meant very much to me through the years. It's found in 2 Chronicles. The fourteenth chapter begins the story of the reign of King Asa over Judah. He was twenty-five years old when he ascended to the throne. Shortly after the beginning of his reign, the Ethiopians invaded the land, joining together with a confederacy of other nations with an army of a million men plus chariots. When Asa received the report of this huge invading army, he prayed unto the Lord and said, "LORD, it is nothing with thee to help, whether with many, or with them that have no power: help us, O LORD our God; for we rest on thee, and in thy name we go against this multitude. O LORD, thou art our God; let not man prevail against thee." (2 Chronicles 14:11).

Now, I like this. He wasn't saying, "God, I have a plan. Now, I want you to bless the plan." He wasn't saying, "Now God, I have it all figured out. Now, bless our program." It wasn't, "God, get on my side." Instead, it was "God, I'm coming on Your side. In Your name we're going to go out against them. Don't let man prevail against You. They aren't going to prevail against me, because I don't have anything. I don't have any power. But, Lord, that doesn't make any difference to You. I'm going to go out in Your name. Don't let them prevail against You. They can beat me, but don't let them beat You."

This is similar to what Jonathan said. God doesn't need a whole army. God can just do it with one man if

God is wanting to work. It's what Paul said in Romans 8:31, "If God be for us, who can be against us."

God gave Asa the victory over the Ethiopians. As Asa was coming back, the prophet of the Lord came out to meet him, and the Lord said through the prophet, "Hear ye me, Asa, and all Judah and Benjamin; The LORD is with you, while ye be with him; and if ye seek him, he will be found of you; but if ye forsake him, he will forsake you." (2 Chronicles 15:2). As he began his reign as king over Judah, Asa received a great word from the Lord. "The Lord will be with you as long as you be with Him. If you seek Him, He will be available. He will be found of you. But, if you forsake Him, He will forsake you."

Under the reign of Asa, the kingdom was prosperous and the people were blessed. But toward the latter part of his reign, when he was wealthy and prosperous and successful, the northern kingdom of Israel decided to invade Judah. They began to build fortified cities north of Jerusalem. They prepared to set up a siege prior to attacking Judah.

When Asa saw them building their fortified cities, he realized what their plan was and took money out of the temple treasury. He sent it to Ben-Hadad, the king of Syria, to hire the Syrians to attack Israel from the north. The Syrians came down from the Golan Heights and began to attack the northern part of Israel. The king of Israel then had to take the troops that were building the fortified cities and deploy them northward to defend against this attack by the Syrians. As the troops left the fortified cities, the men of Judah went out and dismantled the cities.

Looking at the outcome, it seems that the strategy was successful. It worked. Asa was no doubt smug and enjoying his brilliant strategy. Money can do wonderful things, and he was glorying in what you can do if you have enough money. You can hire the Syrians. They're mercenaries, and you can protect yourself. What a successful strategy!

Hanani the prophet came out to Asa and said to him, "Because thou hast relied on the king of Syria, and not relied on the LORD thy God, therefore is the host of the king of Syria escaped out of thine hand. Were not the Ethiopians and the Lubims a huge host, with very many chariots and horsemen? Yet, because thou didst rely on the LORD, he delivered them into thine hand." (2 Chronicles 16:7-8). When you were little and had no strength and were faced with the invading army of the Ethiopians, you trusted in the Lord and the Lord delivered you. Your trust was in Him. But now that you've grown powerful and strong, you're trusting in your own devices. Don't you know that "the eyes of the LORD run to and fro throughout the whole earth, to shew himself strong in the behalf of them whose heart is perfect toward him." (2 Chronicles 16:9). That's the key. The eyes of the Lord are going to and fro throughout the entire earth to find men whose hearts are in harmony with His so that He might show Himself strong in their behalf.

What the prophet is saying is that God wants to work. God has a work that He desires to do, and God is simply looking for people who are in harmony with what He desires in order that He might show Himself strong on their behalf. The key is to discover what it is that God wants to do. I've found that the best way is by just stepping out. Try it and see. Maybe God will work. Maybe God is wanting to work. Let's give Him a chance. But again, always have the attitude "If it doesn't work, let's not push it." Maintain that flexibility of being able to walk away from a project. If it's obvious that it isn't working, then let's not push it and try and make it work.

We see the same idea in the story of Esther when Mordecai told her to go in and see the king. She said,

"You just don't go in and see him. You must be called. You're putting your life on the line to go in if you're not called." Mordecai replied, "You think that if this decree goes through, that you're going to escape? Maybe God has risen you up for such a time as this. If you fail, deliverance will arise in another quarter."

In other words, God's going to do His work. God's going to accomplish His purposes. The nation of Israel can't be wiped out, because it's through them that the Messiah is going to come. You must have the confidence that God's purposes will stand. Though you fail, deliverance will arise from another quarter. God will do the work, but we have the opportunity to be the vessels through which God works. I believe that's often the case. God's got a work that He desires to do. He wants to do it and you can choose to be a participant. You can be the vessel if you dare. With Esther, it was a daring thing to go in uncalled by the king. If he doesn't raise the scepter, she immediately gets killed.

Several years ago there was a book written called, "The Gospel Blimp." It was so typical of the church programs that are devised by men to try to build a church's attendance. It's amazing to see all of the church growth programs, devices, and schemes that people can buy into. The idea was to get this little blimp and to put an invitation to attend the church on the blimp. They then put it on a cable and let it just fly above the church. The idea was to let people know that the church was there. They even put the message, "Jesus Loves You" on the blimp.

The problems that they had keeping that thing up make for a classic story. Finally a storm came and the men were out there trying to hold the thing. They got into a big fight with each other, and it ultimately split the church. Half the people left, angry at the other half. That's so true of man's efforts! Rather than bringing gain to the church, they incurred a loss. Early on, when they saw the thing wasn't working, they said,

"Oh, but we spent fifteen hundred dollars for this blimp. We have to keep it up there." They should have said it was a mistake, forgotten it, and let the thing blow away in the wind. Let's not try to hold onto what God is wanting to blow away.

Several years ago I went down to Lubbock, Texas to speak at a Southern Baptist Church. The pastor said they had decided that they weren't going to keep any program alive in the church by artificial means. In other words, they weren't going to put on life support systems and try to keep things alive that were dying.

This is the mistake that the church has so frequently made. There's a time when God uses a particular kind of a program, but then that time passes. Unfortunately, it's become a tradition for people to try to keep it alive. They pump life support systems into it and attempt to keep it going. With God's help we learn to let things die a natural death instead of trying to keep things going by artificial means.

It's always a sign of degeneration when you have to go back to the past to say what God has done, rather than being able to say, "Look at what God is doing today." Instead of just hearing what God has done, it's important that we become a vital part of the work. We need to experience and see the work of God for ourselves. Otherwise, it won't go on. We need to make each succeeding generation a first generation as far as the experience of the work of God is concerned. In that way, it's being continued. But when we build a memorial and start saying, "Look at what God did, and how God used this person. Look at how God has blessed that man!", be careful. When we build a monument to remind ourselves of what God did in the past, that's always a sad day, because we each need to experience the work of God alive and fresh in our own lives.

There was a time when God was using the Saturday night concerts at Calvary Chapel in just a glorious way. Saturday night concerts were the greatest evangelistic tool that we had going. The place was jammed on Saturday nights. We had a lot of bands and hundreds of kids coming forward to accept Jesus Christ every Saturday night. If you took a poll in Southern California on where people were saved, you'd find that many were saved at a Saturday night concert at Calvary Chapel. There was a time that God was using these concerts, but then that time passed. A couple of years ago, there were some who said that they wanted to try Saturday Night Concerts again. So, I said, "O.K., go for it." But the time had passed. For a while they tried to keep them going, but it was as if God had said, "No, that era is over." Now that doesn't mean that it won't come again sometime, but rather than going on and on and seeing the thing slowly lose its life, it's best to cancel it. Let it go. Let it die. Don't try and keep it going.

So, take a step in faith. If it works, rejoice. If it doesn't, look for something else. Give God the opportunity. I believe strongly in giving God an opportunity, and when it works, glorious! But when it doesn't work, you haven't really gotten that deeply into it so that you can't just walk away and say, "Well, it sure looked like a great idea, didn't it?" Don't lock yourself on to it and get yourself in so deep that you can't walk away.

Be led by the Spirit and don't be afraid to follow. And having begun in the Spirit, don't seek to be made perfect in the flesh. I do see this as a problem, even among some of the guys that were with us at the beginning. God has blessed their ministry, but unfortunately they've gotten much more organized. They're now beginning to direct the program and with it they're losing something that's vital. Having begun in the Spirit, don't seek to be perfected in the flesh. It's always a mistake.

I thank God that He has given us a lot of pastors who caught this vision of simply venturing out in faith. I watch them as they're making these ventures in faith. It's a thrill to see how God is blessing when we dare to step out and allow Him to do what He wants to do, giving ourselves over as instruments through which He can do what He wants to do if He so desires. The key is making ourselves available. So, who knows, the eyes of the Lord are still going to and fro throughout the entire earth to show Himself strong on behalf of those whose hearts are perfect towards Him. Discover the will of God and then jump into it. Get your heart in harmony with His, and you will be amazed at what God will do and how God will bless.

BOOKS BY CHUCK SMITH

LIVING WATER
This book captures the message of
God's ability to change lives through His
Holy Spirit. The reader will grow deeply in
the knowledge and understanding of the
Holy Spirit; His grace, His love, His
power, and His gifts. 297 pages.

WHY GRACE
CHANGES EVERYTHING
Through remarkable insight gleaned
from the Bible and his own life, Pastor Chuck
unfolds the mystery of grace. The reader will
be refreshed and encouraged by the depth
of God's grace toward us. Also available in
Spanish. 218 pages.

ANSWERS FOR TODAY
A compilation of the popular Answer
Pamphlet series, this book includes "It's Time
for the Sunrise," "Questions & Answers,"
"Unto Us a Son Is Given," "A More Sure Word,"
and many others. 183 pages.

TO ORDER CALL 1-800-272-9673

THE FINAL CURTAIN

This recently updated book deals with such subjects as Bible prophecy, the Middle East, Russia, and the role of the Antichrist. Also included is a helpful glossary with terms relating to the Bible and prophecy. 96 pages.

THE GOSPEL ACCORDING TO GRACE

A clear and enlightening commentary on the Book of Romans. Chuck Smith reviews Paul's epistle, one of the most important books in the Bible, on a verse-by-verse basis. 164 pages.

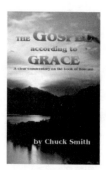

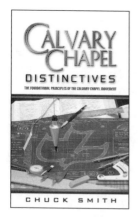

CALVARY CHAPEL DISTINCTIVES

Calvary Chapel values both the teaching of God's Word, as well as the work of the Holy Spirit. It is this balance that makes Calvary Chapel a distinct and uniquely blessed movement of God. 250 pages.

EFFECTIVE PRAYER LIFE
This practical study in prayer will
equip and help you to have a more
effective and dynamic prayer life. An
excellent resource for personal growth and
group discipleship. 99 pages.

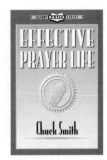

HARVEST
Pastors from ten Calvary Chapels share
how God broke through the barriers of
evil, pride, and anger to carry out His
plan. Many insights into evangelizing
and trusting God's Word make this book
a valuable resource for every believer.
160 pages.

TRIBULATION AND THE CHURCH
Will the church of Christ experience the
Tribulation? This book expounds upon biblical
prophecy and future events while looking
at the role the church will play. 72 pages.

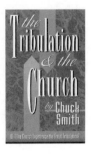

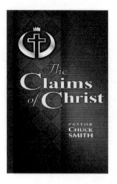

THE CLAIMS OF CHRIST
Chuck Smith gives a straightforward presentation of the claims of Jesus Christ, along with proof of their validity. Readers are challenged to accept or reject the claims of Christ. 16 pages.

WHAT THE WORLD IS COMING TO
This book is a complete commentary on the book of Revelation and the scenario for the last days. Our world is coming to an end fast, but you don't have to go down with it! 215 pages.

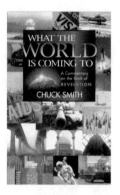

1 JOHN NOTES
Excellent for pastors or students! Taken from Chuck Smith's personal study notes, this can be used as an outline for Bible study groups, Sunday school classes, or individual studies. First John is explored verse-by-verse, with cross-referencing to other books of the Bible. 66 pages.

LET US HELP YOU 1-800-272-WORD

COMFORT
FOR THOSE WHO MOURN
In this pamphlet, Pastor Chuck shares
the glorious hope we have in the
resurrection of Jesus Christ and how
we can find comfort through Him
during a time of loss. 15 pages.

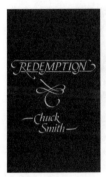

REDEMPTION
In this clear and easy to read commentary,
Pastor Chuck explores and explains the
concept of our redemption in Christ using as
background the story of Ruth and her "Goel"
or savior, Boaz. 16 pages.

CHRISTIAN FAMILY
RELATIONSHIPS
Christian Family Relationships reveals
God's basic principles designed to keep your
family's love alive. By knowing and applying
God's principles to your family life, you can
have real peace, happiness, and joy. 68 pages.

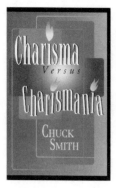

CHARISMA VS. CHARISMANIA
Chuck Smith explores the "charismatic experience," a theological controversy that has existed for years. A wonderful book for those seeking to find a balanced relationship with the Holy Spirit. 146 pages.

THE SEARCH FOR MESSIAH
Written by Dr. Mark Eastman & Chuck Smith, this book is a gateway of discovery for the serious pilgrim in search of the Messiah. The skeptic will be challenged and the Christian deeply enriched. 276 pages.

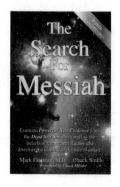

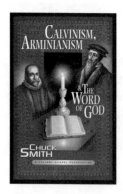

CALVINISM, ARMINIANISM & THE WORD OF GOD
This pamphlet discusses the facts upon which these two doctrinal stands are based, and compares them to the Word of God. 8 pages.

OUR OPERATORS ARE STANDING BY 1-800-272-WORD

TAPE PACKS BY CHUCK SMITH

MOST REQUESTED TAPE PACK
This tape pack contains twelve of the most
requested Bible studies by Pastor Chuck.
Some messages included are: Faith that
prevails; How can a man be born again;
Trusting in lies, and many more.
12 messages.

**PROPHECY UPDATE
2001 TAPE PACK**
What are the implications of the recent
events in Israel? Are the pieces of the puzzle
finally coming together, leading to a one-
world government? Pastor Chuck examines
these issues in a timely series. In-depth commentaries on prophetic Scripture passages
are also included. 4 messages.

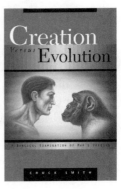

CREATION VS. EVOLUTION TAPE PACK
Pastor Chuck Smith hosts a collection of
biblical studies that focus on the validity of
Creation and the scientific evidence that
backs it up. Besides Pastor Chuck, the
following guests are included: Chuck
Missler, Roger Oakland, Dr. Mark Eastman
and Dr. Henry Morris. 10 messages.

FOR FRIENDLY SERVICE 1-800-272-9673

GOD'S WAKE UP CALL TAPE PACK

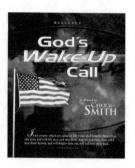

Beginning with a heartfelt prayer delivered by Pastor Chuck on Sept. 11, 2001, this tape pack will help the listener understand God's purpose and plan for our nation. 6 messages.

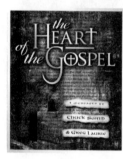

THE HEART OF THE GOSPEL TAPE PACK

Have you ever wondered what it means to be born again or why Jesus' resurrection is crucial to the Christian faith? Or maybe you wanted to share your faith with others, but weren't sure how. By Pastors Chuck Smith & Greg Laurie. 4 messages.

ISRAEL TAPE PACK

This tape pack studies the richness of the Hebrew culture and homeland; from their feasts to their covenants with God. Ten biblical studies by Pastor Chuck Smith, Chuck Missler, Brian Brodersen, Dave Hunt, and David Hocking. 10 messages.

LET US HELP YOU 1-800-272-WORD

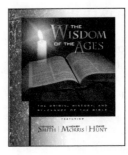

THE WISDOM OF THE AGES
TAPE PACK
Pastor Chuck Smith, Dr. Henry Morris, and Dave Hunt discuss the most reliable Bible translations, the basis for our Bible, as well as the inerrancy, sufficiency, and authority of the scriptures.
4 messages.

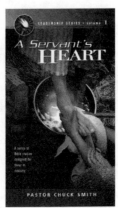

A SERVANT'S HEART TAPE PACK
Whether you teach Sunday school to a classroom of five-year olds, or lead worship for a congregation of five thousand, the Lord has a special plan for your life. This tape pack focuses on the nature of a servant, as well as the requirements necessary to follow the Lord.
7 messages.

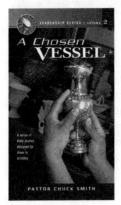

A CHOSEN VESSEL TAPE PACK
How can we better prepare ourselves to be used by the Lord? This tape pack encourages and guides those in ministry, preparing them for the work set before them. This collection focuses on the tools necessary to be a leader.
7 messages.

TO PLACE AN ORDER CALL 1-800-272-9673

MARRIAGE & FAMILY TAPE PACK
Volumes 1 & 2
Discusses the blessing of personal relationships, how to mend bad relationships, the importance of training our children, and scriptural duties of husbands and wives.
Volume 1 has 6 messages.
Volume 2 has 7 messages.

MY REDEEMER LIVES TAPE PACK
This collection of 8 tapes contains 14 Old & New Testament Bible studies. It covers the death and resurrection of Jesus Christ: From the fulfillment of prophetic scriptures to the proof of the resurrection. 14 messages.

STANDING UP IN
A FALLEN WORLD TAPE PACK
Based on the Book of Daniel, these messages were recorded during a youth camp. Each tape contains a powerful message for today's young generation. Suitable for those between the ages of 12 - 20. A study guide is also available. 4 messages.

OUR OPERATORS ARE STANDING BY 1-800-272-WORD

THE PERSON OF THE
HOLY SPIRIT TAPE PACK
This set explains who the Holy Spirit is
and how He works. 12 messages.

THE GIFTS OF THE
HOLY SPIRIT TAPE PACK
This tape pack covers such subjects as
miracles, healing, prophecy, faith and
speaking in tongues. 19 messages.

TIDINGS OF GREAT JOY TAPE PACK
Do you know the prophecies that were
fulfilled in Jesus' birth and death, and why they
had to take place? Do you know why a man
born 2,000 years ago can still affect our world?
Interestingly, it all began in the Garden of Eden.
4 messages.

To order any of our products or to receive a free catalog,
please call us at
1-800-272-WORD

Or write to us at
THE WORD FOR TODAY
P.O. Box 8000
Costa Mesa, CA 92628

FOR FRIENDLY SERVICE   1-800-272-9673